NVENTION IN PR

ADAM RITCHIE

"Despite the fact that earned media has never been more effective or necessary for brand storytelling and communication, PR pros still struggle to convince stakeholders they are the natural creative firestarters. But, at its best, PR is essentially an ideas business. Adam Ritchie's *Invention in PR* gives you a jump-start to stimulating creativity and coming up with inventive activations that really move the needle and make audiences care."

– **PRWeek** *Editorial Director Steve Barrett*

"By putting invention at the top of PR's to-do list, Adam Ritchie has fundamentally flipped the industry's charge from promoting the products and services clients already have, to creating them. Ritchie has made a successful go of doing just that, and in *Invention in PR* he instructively lays out the reasoning for his signature approach to PR, and ways of making it work. The book is a must-read for the gamut of people in the communications business: as thought-provoking for newcomers wanting to make their mark, as for industry vets looking to mix things up."

– **PRovoke** *Senior Reporter Diana Marszalek*

"After reading a few pages of *Invention in PR*, you'll realize there are at least two reasons why it's not like other PR books. First, Adam Ritchie is a realist. He admits up-front that the case studies and examples most of us read in PR books are 'highly polished, written for future clients, awards judges and textbooks.' They rarely include hurdles faced or mistakes made. As such, they don't resemble PR in the real world, where as Adam writes, 'Even the most lauded campaigns are a series of secret battles lost and won, internally and externally. Nothing falls into place.' Adam offers examples of how PR pros overcome obstacles so they can make things fall into place. And second, this book is different because Adam's ideas about PR are evolutionary. Adam felt PR could do more than promote companies and their products. Instead, Adam thought PR could create products that would earn media. Of course, Adam knows his thinking about PR pros creating products is unconventional.

Let your mind roam. Consider his arguments. The results could be invigorating."

– **PR News** *Editor Seth Arenstein*

"For PR and communications pros looking to stop taking orders and become essential business advisors, Adam Ritchie's book is a must-read collection of case studies and career lessons for making a PR campaign an intrinsic part of the enterprise. In example after award-winning example, Ritchie offers a fresh perspective on creative PR work, where communicators are in the driver's seat and their inventiveness and business-savvy provide the keys to earning recognition from top decision-makers."

– **PR Daily** *Editor Ted Kitterman*

"This book is filled with wonderful examples of true creativity and ingenuity. Adam Ritchie is a bona fide out-of-the-box thinker, and it has been a pleasure to follow his work over the years and consistently recognize him for these superbly crafted successful campaigns. There are myriad examples included here that speak to his clever planning and execution, which truly define PR success in the modern era. I recommend this brilliant book to PR practitioners young and old. There are valuable lessons and actionable takeaways for all."

– **Bulldog Reporter** *Editor Richard Carufel*

"Getting Adam Ritchie's creative brain into a book is akin to catching lightning in a bottle, only less dangerous and far more electric. Energize your next PR campaign with inspiration from this volume of true stories!"

– **PR Nation** *Host Robert Johnson*

"It is far too common for PR professionals to be shut out of key decision making, often coming into projects too late to make a difference. This is a detriment not only to PR professionals and the industry, but also to various projects and organizations as a whole. Adam Ritchie's *Invention in PR* is the first book to serve such a unique antidote to this important issue. His account of how PR can help shape product development is revolutionary."

– **PR Talk** *Host Amy Rosenberg*

"Once you read this book, it is impossible to think about PR in the same way ever again. It can have more meaning and substance than you might have believed. I loved the narrative of taking charge of your destiny through original ideas, and pushing back on boring, stuffy client briefs that have you acting as a fulfillment service – as opposed to pushing boundaries and making history. The quote that resonated with me the most was, 'Innovation streamlines the arrow. Invention creates the bullet.' Definitely going to use that one. And as a Scottish person, a bonus was the Loch Ness Monster even getting a mention!"

– **The Drum** *Managing Director of Events Lynn Lester*

"Adam Ritchie is an iconoclast and nonconformist in an industry that gets advanced and built by iconoclasts and nonconformists. It's easy to play it safe and follow industry or client norms, but Adam is smart enough to recognize that creativity thrives in discomfort. His book is a peak into that thought process,and provides a roadmap to break through and disrupt in a sea of sameness."

– **Molson Coors Beverage Company**
President, Emerging Growth Pete Marino

"Adam Ritchie has a passion for PR and a unique gift as a storyteller with an edgy style. I love bringing something new and different to the table. He wrote the book – literally this book – on bringing something new and different to the table. I have seen him speak about Invention in PR many times throughout my career, and every time I learn something new. His bold and fierce approach to PR is refreshing, timely and unique to him. His guidance, advice and case studies are something every communicator, student and organization should know and apply to their campaigns. Personally, he is

ne of the kindest, most compassionate people I know. He is
lso one of the smartest people I know. From his parents, to his
ollege roommate, to his former interns, they all say the same
hing: Adam is simply Adam. A curious, genius, hard-worker
who helps those in need. I am so proud of my dear friend and
'R colleague Adam Ritchie for what he has accomplished and
ontinues to accomplish. I hope everyone who reads this book
ets inspired, empowered and brings a little invention to their
able."

– IBM
Manager, Digital and Advocacy Communications
Brandi Boatner

'Your first trigger pull should always be aimed at the
udacious.' When I read that sentence, it brought me back
o my first introduction to Adam Ritchie, when I knew
e possessed a level of creativity, wisdom and intelligence
eyond his years. Nearly two decades later, he has gone on to
ip the industry on its head with *Invention in PR*. Endlessly
alented in music and PR, he is a unique risk-taker grounded
1 knowledge of human behavior and informed by research
n society and trends. He is one of the most hard-working,
erseverant people I've ever met. All of those attributes are
vhat make his case studies and insights within the book
1valuable. *Invention in PR* is informative and inspiring for
ny PR, marketing or communications practitioner who
vants to move beyond staid strategies and tactics. I highly
ecommend it for pros who want a peek into the work
f Adam Ritchie Brand Direction and its founder, whose
1ventive work has won every award in the industry."

– New Balance
Global Community Outreach Manager Amy Sweeney

Adam Ritchie offers us the valuable cheat codes to the
uture of PR, showing how we can have as much influence on
roduct development as we do on product promotion."
– Dunkin' *Vice President, Communications Glen Schwartz*

"The *Invention in PR* approach is a completely new roadmap that is bold, brave and needed in a world where it's never been harder to break through the clutter. It redefines and repositions PR's role across a product's journey into consumers' hands, hearts and minds."
 – **ViacomCBS Velocity** *Executive Vice President Chris Ficarr*

"*Invention in PR* is a testament to the true core of creativity by an author with a healthy and irreverent disregard for the status quo, who refuses to let a label or job description prescribe how he approaches a challenge."
– JPMorgan Chase & Co
Vice President, User Experience Design Lead Katie Dadarra

"*Invention in PR* is a refreshing take on public relations that goes beyond traditional tactics and presents a better way of thinking about the value PR pros provide."
– LEGO Educatio
Digital Engagement Lead Amanda Fountar

"*Invention in PR* made me re-excited about the industry and its future. I wish I could invent a time machine and take it back to my 22-year-old self, so she could read it and absolutel crush it for every client she touched. This book made me thinl of PR in a new light: not simply putting out fires or generating coverage, but generating true art. It should be part of every PI curriculum, with the caveat that the professor has to rappel into the first class from 50 feet in the air, wearing light-up gea It also talks about failures, prepares readers for unavoidable snags and shows how some of the best in the biz can break th rules, but always do it above-board."
– Akama
Senior Manager, Corporate Communications Brenda Manaco

"With *Invention in PR*, Adam Ritchie liberates the public relations profession and frees us from coloring within the lines. It's PR's manual for going from the safety of the back seat to driving the yellow Ferrari through a red light at 90 miles per hour. Ritchie doesn't consider himself a creative, saying, 'You don't get to pin that on yourself.' Well, I'm pinning it him. He's our industry's Albert Einstein – in a leather jacket."

– Takeda
U.S. Neuroscience and Commercial Operations Communications Lead Monique Kelley Gigliotti

"What do you think the future of PR looks like? Adam Ritchie does it again and pushes the limits with *Invention in PR*. Ritchie offers a refreshing new perspective that approaches PR as a means of invention, flipping traditional ideas upside down."

– Public Relations Society of America
Director, Professional Development Jason Barnhart

"Adam Ritchie's invention-first focus on the discipline presents an inspiring and expansive way of thinking about the creativity that is core to what we do."

– PR Council *President Kim Sample*

"Adam Ritchie doesn't sugarcoat the challenges in his fast-moving guide to three pillars of success all public relations professionals should know, but are rarely taught: invention, creation and transformation. Guided by stories and lessons from his career, Ritchie shares action-oriented steps to turn his practical recommendations into habits for success."

– Institute for Public Relations
President and Chief Executive Officer Tina McCorkindale

"Betsy Plank, a pioneering practitioner, once said that viewing PR in the narrow sense of simply publicizing new products and product improvements is a myopic attitude that will continue to relegate public relations to an also-ran in marketing strategy and budgeting. She went on to say that public relations must be directed toward the consumer's self-interest, not just that of the company or brand. With such an approach, public relations practitioners would be positioned to sense, analyze, interpret and influence the consumers marketers were trying to reach. And public relations planning would move from an after-the-fact consideration to a place of authority and respect early in the marketing strategy development. Plank made her comments back in 1968, but her words did not produce much change. Not that is, until Adam Ritchie came along. Like Plank, Ritchie sees a broader role for public relations, one he calls *Invention in PR*. His book is a clarion call for practitioners. He says it's time we exercised our creative muscles and go beyond simply publicizing new products and become a source of invention and transformation. His book is highly readable, full of real-world examples and he keeps it real-world. He shows that taking a campaign from concept to implementation is not easy, but when it all comes together, it is magical. I can't wait to assign this book to my students. All practitioners involved with marketing and media need to read *Invention in PR* to be reinvigorated and inspired."

– Plank Center for Leadership in Public Relations
Director Karla Gower

"Adam Ritchie is a rare talent and beyond brilliant. Soak up every bit of knowledge he's dispensing and you'll be a better PR professional. And you'll be more than entertained by the great stories he tells in pursuit of bringing the passion he has for his work to life. This is a must-read."

– Arthur W. Page Society *Chairman Charlene Wheeless*

"*Invention in PR* is a bold and no holds barred approach to building campaigns that will inspire every reader, no matter their stage of experience."
– The Museum of Public Relations *Co-Founder Shelley Spector*

"'Where has your work taken you today?' is a brilliant question posed by Adam Ritchie. If you are in PR, this book will encourage – no, insist – that your work doesn't start at the end of product development. Your role must spark new, better or transformational offerings. Period. If you need

practical guidance, motivation or a kick in the ass to rethink your role as a PR professional, this book will give you a healthy dose of each."
– **Content Marketing Institute** *General Manager Stephanie Stahl*

"Adam Ritchie has always been a pioneer in our field, and *Invention in PR* is a useful, fun read packed with practical advice and inspiring case studies that remind us how to love what we do. I look forward to seeing all the inventions this book is sure to spark!"
– **Edelman** *Senior Vice President Anne Erhard*

"*Invention in PR* is not an abstract or academic read. Learning comes from doing, and Adam Ritchie invites you to ride along on a career's worth of discovery."
– **Weber Shandwick** *Executive Creative Director Jenna Young*

"While this book is theoretically about PR Invention, it's really a book about the new expectations for brand creativity. Because how good can a 'big idea' really be if it's not driving media conversation? Today's best, most award-winning creative ideas are inherently newsworthy. PR is baked into them from the very beginning, not bolted on at the very end. The PR industry has been saying this for decades, yet most PR people have let their creativity be beaten out of them by best practices and swim lanes. Adam Ritchie is showing an entire generation it's possible to be both an amazing PR professional AND an amazing creative. Read this book and then walk into your next brainstorming meeting with the confidence that not only does PR deserve a seat at that table – it should also be the one leading the conversation."
– **BCW Global** *Senior Vice President Steve Radick*

"Adam Ritchie takes us through a PR revolution where our minds are tuned to the role of inventor and we bring more value to our clients."
– **FleishmanHillard** *Senior Vice President Seth Bloom*

"Adam Ritchie is one of the most unique and talented voices in PR. His limitless energy and determination to rethink traditional communications have earned him a seat at the product strategy table."

— **Porter Novelli** *Executive Vice President Heather Breslau*

"It's impossible to read this book and not have your head swirling with ideas. Adam Ritchie is a fountain of creativity and inspiration. His breakdown of the inventive PR process makes it accessible for anyone to push their limits and challenge themselves to create truly novel communications campaigns. *Invention in PR* is a quick read, and well worth every moment."

— **Allison+Partners** *Executive Vice President Paul Breton*

"Adam Ritchie delivers a nontraditional and transformative view of PR's full potential. *Invention in PR* is for professionals considering what's next, and where the product ideas of the future will originate."

— **Zeno Group** *Managing Director Byron Calamese*

"The advice Adam Ritchie shares in these pages will guide us into the next phase of PR's evolution."

— **Ruder Finn** *Chief Executive Officer Kathy Bloomgarden*

"Adam Ritchie has written an inspiring book with brilliant insight and examples of how in this industry, creativity is a given, but great success is found in being inventive."

— **M Booth**
Senior Vice President, Entertainment Marketing and Partnerships Michelle Overall

"I love Adam Ritchie's *Invention in PR* because it is a quick, one-sitting read which captures what I find magical about our profession. Adam has essentially made a taxonomy for invention and creativity in PR."

— **PadillaCRT** *Co-Founder Patrice Tanaka*

Adam Ritchie has written a fun, useful and inspiring guide or using PR to truly create."

– Carmichael Lynch *President Julie Batliner*

It's one thing to compile the PR industry's greatest hits. It's nother to present interesting archetypes and a powerful pproach by examining brands of all sizes. In example after xample of what happens when the imagination gear is fully ngaged in public relations, *Invention in PR* encourages us ll to twist the lens in new ways. While many of us look up nd see clouds, Adam Ritchie is one of those people who sees antastic creatures and stories in the sky."

– Fahlgren Mortine
Executive Vice President Marty McDonald

Adam Ritchie has always been one step ahead in this fast-aced industry of ours. Anything he writes is a must-read."

– PAN Communications
President and Chief Executive Officer Philip Nardone

Adam Ritchie is one of the few professionals to go beyond reat PR and consistently deliver transformative PR. *nvention in PR* is an essential resource for breaking out of ommunication ruts and looking at things in a new way."

– C+C *General Manager Mark McClennan*

I wish I had written this. Adam Ritchie's new work has given ne a true case of professional envy!"

– Bospar *Principal Curtis Sparrer*

Adam Ritchie has the audacity to not just think outside the ox; he's throwing out the box and showing us a whole new vay. Using the muscles and disciplines of PR, he's seizing our noment to drive true invention. The time is now and Ritchie sn't waiting. Neither should we."

– Salient Global
Chief Executive Officer and former Olson Engage President
Bryan Specht

"I haven't been this freaking jazzed about PR since I first started in the industry more than 20 years ago. Adam Ritchie's unique approach to PR is exactly what the industry needs after spending many years in the shadows of the advertisers. After decades of PR agencies simply being asked to amplify whatever oddity the ad agency wanted to put out, the tables are turning. We are increasingly seeing brands open the floor to all agencies to come up with the lead creative idea. The best idea wins, period! And as Ritchie points out, rethinking the role of PR through the lens of invention gives us the opportunity to seize the day."

– **Brodeur Partners** *Executive Vice President Scott Beaudoin*

"Adam Ritchie is challenging the industry to write stories, which is more powerful than only telling them."

– **Matter Communications** *Vice President Monica Higgins*

"*Invention in PR* is relatable and fresh thinking. Adam Ritchie takes complicated concepts and breaks them down into an easily-digestible roadmap that elevates the PR discipline."

– **Kite Hill** *Chief Executive Officer Tiffany Guarnaccia*

"Adam Ritchie's *Invention in PR* codifies a proven approach for brands large and small to creatively break through the noise, punch above their weight class and drive business results. Life's too short for boring ideas. Invent something!"

– **Fallon** *Head of Creative Innovation Greg Swan*

"What a read! Adam Ritchie's commitment to teaching and growing the philosophy of PR as a product and service inventor can help usher in a new era."

– **MGH**
Chief Operating Officer
and Director of Public Relations and Account Management
Chris McMurry

"If the field of public relations were to hire a publicist, it would be well-served to retain Adam Ritchie. *Invention in PR* is both an apt title and one that can't help but fall short of describing what awaits the reader. This is in no small part due to Ritchie's novel insights into a skill I've always found near-impossible to explain, despite spending 30-plus years doing it! Thankfully, with *Invention in PR*, someone has risen to the task of unlocking the mysteries of the amorphous entity that's paid my bills all these years. Ritchie's come so far, but in a way he's still working from the same location: the intersection of passion and creativity. It's no easy place to reach, but *Invention in PR* is as close as you're likely to come to a guide."

– **Nasty Little Man** *Founder Steve Martin*

"Adam Ritchie has written the quintessential modern guide to PR. *Invention in PR* transcends the standard how-to by offering vibrant, often personal anecdotes of Ritchie's incredibly inventive, sometimes off-the-wall, but always impactful campaigns. Fledgling and veteran publicists will come away with loads of inspiration, and brand entrepreneurs will no longer have to doubt the power of thinking to the sides."

– **Vicious Kid Public Relations** *President Perry Serpa*

"Corporate PR can be dry. Adam Ritchie maps out a way for you to stand out while adding real value. His campaigns are fun, helpful to the community and far more interesting than anything you are currently doing. Do as he says, and you'll be doing PR for the next 20 years."

– **The Planetary Group** *Owner Adam Lewis*

"*Invention in PR* is an incredibly conversational and engaging read, as timeless as Edward Bernays himself."

– **Top Hat** *Founder Ben Butler*

"*Invention in PR* is a book every public relations, marketing and advertising professional must read. I have always said, when in crisis, the solution must match the emotional level of the crisis itself to counteract and help put out the crisis fire. Author and PR expert Adam Ritchie gets that emotional intelligence is the greatest tool in the crisis management toolbox. I give *Invention in PR* two Rep Doc thumbs up!"
– **Reputation Doctor** *President Mike Paul*

"Adam Ritchie's highly creative lens on the public relations profession provides the freedom for all practitioners to dream and aspire to more collaborative, inventive relationships with their clients."

– **Image Suite PR**
President, Communications Paula MacDonald

"In an approachable, real-world tone with evergreen content that is of-the-moment without veering into trendy, Adam Ritchie's blueprint for success shares the superpowers that led to his boutique shop becoming a little engine that could in the PR industry."

– **Jill Siegel Communications** *President Jill Siegel*

"Adam Ritchie is a masterful storyteller, and his entrepreneurial approach to solving problems is an adrenaline shot of inspiration with a practical path to making magic happen."

– **Harvard University**
Adjunct Professor Kristian Darigan Merenda

"Adam Ritchie will ignite your passion for PR. Penned by one of the most creative minds in our field, *Invention in PR* reveals how not to take what you're given, but instead to come up with something better. Something better is what this book is all about. It's a great read, an easy read, an exciting read and a motivating read."

– **Syracuse University**
Director, Newhouse Public Diplomacy Program
Dennis Kinsey

"*Invention in PR* brings to life an invaluable framework for developing newsworthy products and services, which helps communication professionals get – and keep – a seat at the leadership table."

– DePaul University
Director, Professional Communication Graduate Program
Matt Ragas

"Adam Ritchie's book redefines PR as a more upstream function where powerful ideas drive invention and impact. The book's typology of the different forms of invention deserves to be widely taught and adopted."

– New York University
Academic Director and Clinical Assistant Professor,
Integrated Marketing and Communications Department
Michael Diamond

"Adam Ritchie's *Invention PR* is just what our profession deserves: an unapologetic and inspiring shot of creative adrenaline. It delights with invention-fueled ideas bursting with soul and audacity. Ritchie invites us to become authors of what our field should be, and have lots of fun along the way."

– Boston University *Professor of Public Relations Steve Quigley*

"It's rare when a book comes along that not only causes me to think about an industry in a totally new way – but also excites me about the possibilities such a new perspective presents. *Invention in PR* did just that for me. Adam Ritchie completely redefines what the PR industry could and should be. The way he views his agency's place and responsibility in the field is something I look forward to sharing with my students who will soon become practitioners themselves. I want them to see themselves as inventors in the way Ritchie describes. I want them to understand that the ideation process isn't always easy or pretty – but it can be extremely rewarding in so many ways. And I want them to always be willing to challenge the status quo so that they'll not only be able to tell – but also write – the very best brand stories for their clients. *Invention in PR* is a must-read for students, seasoned industry professionals and everyone in between. It has certainly reinvented the way I look at what's possible."

– Elon University
Assistant Professor, Strategic Communications Michele Lashley

"For years I used to tell my students you can't invent products – that's not PR. But as Adam Ritchie details with his own experience, and by profiling many brands, inventing new products and services is the exciting frontier of PR."

– American University
Assistant Professor/Senior Associate Director,
Public Communication Division
Pallavi Kumar

"Adam Ritchie's *Invention in PR* promises to set the whole industry on fire and change it forever."

– University of Connecticut
Academic Advisor, Department of Communication
Joel Nebres

"It's rare that I read a PR book and not want to put it down. As I read *Invention in PR*, I kept yelling, 'But what happened next?' and continuing on to the next chapter. You will gain some great, stealable ideas by reading this book."

– Spin Sucks
Author and Creator of the PESO Model® Gini Dietrich

INVENTION IN PR

A handbook for pushing the limits of PR to inventing things, rather than only promoting them. When PR teams live or die on the success or failure of the products and services they support, *Invention in PR* shows how they can take a stronger hand in their creation.

This book says the profession can do better than waiting for someone else to determine, develop and package what a company sells. It spurs PR pros to go beyond what they're handed and come up with new products and services that change a brand's life.

Through tales of award-winning campaigns passionately told by their creator, readers learn how to apply invention at the beginning of the PR process and take away usable strategies and tactics. With PR under constant pressure to evolve, communications pioneer Adam Ritchie uncovers practitioners' aptitude for invention and empowers them to harness it.

For PR professionals ready to rebel against taking a back seat to their counterparts in marketing and advertising, *Invention in PR* teaches them how to beat every other discipline to the punch by coming up with the product or service idea first.

This guide will fire up professionals of all generations about what they can build. It will change the way experienced pros approach their jobs, and inspire students to break the rules in the best possible ways.

Adam Ritchie advocates for public relations to evolve from its past as an organization's mouthpiece to its future as an organization's creative engine. Nationally regarded in the U.S., he's been named the field's most innovative professional (PRovoke), launched campaigns honored as the most creative (PRWeek) and runs a practice recognized as the top boutique agency in the country (PR News). He has won every award in the industry multiple times, presented at dozens of conferences and spoken at more than 50 universities on the topic of this book.

INVENTION IN PR

Adam Ritchie

NEW YORK AND LONDON

Cover image: Creative Outlaw

First published 2022
by Routledge
605 Third Avenue, New York, NY 10158

and by Routledge
4 Park Square, Milton Park, Abingdon, Oxon, OX14 4RN

Routledge is an imprint of the Taylor & Francis Group, an informa business

Library of Congress Cataloging-in-Publication Data
A catalog record for this title has been requested

ISBN: 978-1-032-10751-6 (hbk)
ISBN: 978-1-032-10749-3 (pbk)
ISBN: 978-1-003-21687-2 (ebk)

DOI: 10.4324/9781003216872

Typeset in Bembo
by Newgen Publishing UK

CONTENTS

FOREWORD

"We deal in reality."

– *Edward Bernays, PR pro*[1]

I first met Adam in March of 2019. He had seen The Museum of Public Relations on Google Maps and decided to come by on the spur of a moment. I had given three classes and four tours that week. The last thing I wanted was more visitors, but I figured anyone who makes a point of coming all the way downtown to see a museum on a beautiful spring Friday afternoon is someone who must really love this business.

And boy am I glad I told the front desk that he should come up.

It's said that you make an impression of someone within the first five minutes. I made my impression of Adam within the first five seconds. Instantly, I knew this young man was going places. He was the first visitor to the Museum *ever* to have

ead Edward Bernays's books and understand his theories.
That's a surefire way to my heart.

t seemed to me that his Invention approach was very much
n the spirit of what Bernays engineered nearly a century ago.
Like Bernays, Adam and I believe that PR is much more than
ust a mouthpiece. PR can guide not only how a product is
aunched; it can guide the very way a product is designed.
And by doing that you can make news, quickly rise above
he competition and become very successful in a short period
of time.

Adam has been so successful with this approach that he and
his firm have swept each and every awards competition in the
ndustry: from the PRSA Silver Anvils, to winning PRWeek's
Best in Creative Excellence and to being named by PRovoke
s the Most Innovative Marketing Communications Agency
Professional in the U.S.

Adam has taken his Invention in PR workshop all over the
ountry, encouraging professionals to be more daring, more
reative and more *inventive* in their approach to PR. This
s a very bold and no holds barred approach to building
ampaigns. One that I think will inspire every reader, no
matter your stage of experience.

take great pride in introducing this work by our industry's
tar inventor, Adam Ritchie.

Shelley Spector
Co-Founder, The Museum of Public Relations

NOTE

Stuart Ewen's introduction to *Crystallizing Public Opinion* (Open
Road Media, 2015, first published in 1923).

AUTHOR'S NOTE

"We all need to give back to the things that are important to us in our lives."

– Thom Ritchie, Volunteer

You don't need me to teach you how to pitch.

Every PR pro has their tricks. Anyone could write that book as well as me. A lot of them already have.

The last time I was asked to speak about it, I didn't feel like pulling together the world's thousandth "How to Pitch" deck. When you volunteer your time, you should get to choose where it goes. I decided it would be more fun and helpful to put together a session on using PR to drive product development. I called the talk "Invention in PR" and told the event organizers I'd be doing that instead.

It went over well enough that I wanted to teach it everywhere. In the three years that followed, I gave the talk a

51 individual schools to 1,674 students, and at five national conferences to 384 professionals.[2] When surveyed, every educator who booked a session said it inspired their students and changed what they believed PR could accomplish. More than half of them said they saw a direct impact on their subsequent work.[3] One student attendee said the material was "literally changing the way I think."[4] One professional attendee said it "made me think about things in a new way that pushes me, and the profession, forward."[5]

Sometimes when you're asked for an apple, you can offer up an apple pie. That's the attitude behind this approach. Don't take what you're given. Come up with something better.

The more I preached it, the more I practiced it. It solidified my firm's approach to PR. Near the end of the tour, we evolved our positioning to become the only agency in the world using PR as an unstoppable source of invention and transformation. We set out to inspire a wave of practitioners, and along the way uncovered our own singular focus and purpose as a business.

I've condensed what resonated from those talks into one volume for PR pros and students. In these chapters, we'll define the different types of Inventions in PR, look at real-world examples, explore what went into them and share habits anyone can adopt to mine this vein. It's a niche within a niche. Business > Public Relations > Creativity > Invention. If you're here, then like Shelley Spector says, you must really love PR.

Most case studies we consume are highly polished, written for future clients, awards judges and textbooks. Campaign sizzle reels make the work appear seamless. In reality, it's never easy. Forces conspire to keep you from reaching your objectives. Even the most lauded campaigns are a series of secret battles lost and won, internally and externally. Nothing falls into place. You make things fall into place.

This book is about one way of getting things to fall into place while making life exciting for you and the brands you serve.

I hope you'll gain a feel for using your PR skills to create newsworthy products and services, constructing campaigns that cross industries and continents, developing strategies and tactics tied directly to business outcomes, blurring the line between pixels and print and merging the digital with the physical. At the very least, we'll get your gears turning with an approach that turns the idea of PR on its head.

I'd like to ignite or reinvigorate your passion for PR by pushing it beyond existing definitions, and show you how to convert seemingly impossible communications challenges into some of the most fun you'll have in your career.

Thank you for joining me. Let's go make something.

Adam Ritchie
Principal, Adam Ritchie Brand Direction

NOTES

1 Thom Ritchie in an email to Adam Ritchie (January 12, 2009).
2 Adam Ritchie Brand Direction. "Invention." http://aritchbrand.com/invention
3 Adam Ritchie Brand Direction. "Invention in PR – Campaign Sizzle Reel (Official)" (YouTube). http://youtu.be/LLLJSHNWIGQ
4 Tweet from BYU Idaho Student Mackenzie Holbrook (October 8, 2017). http://twitter.com/the_mac_attackk/status/917052553061421059
5 Evaluation from anonymous "Invention in PR" attendee at the IABC World Conference (June 15, 2020).

PROLOGUE

"I don't fit in anywhere I go, but I belong everywhere I am."
– Kenn Elmore, Educator[1]

Some things they don't prepare you for in PR school.

Like being hoisted up into the darkness by a cherry picker on the launch night of a big campaign. Or jumping out of it and rappelling onto a stage covered in lasers and fog.

My crew and I were crammed into a tiny metal basket. Two of us were giddy. One of us was petrified, so we made him line up third so he wouldn't chicken out. The last one was nervous but game, so we tasked him with making the third guy jump.

The mechanical arm started to rise.

20 feet. 30 feet.

This time I wasn't just the publicist. I was also the client. The people on that mechanical lift weren't just my team members. They were also my bandmates. More than a year earlier, we started on the trail of an idea which led to this stunt that was literally a stunt.

40 feet. 50 feet.

Earlier in the day when I suggested we descend onto the stage from a giant swirling wormhole projected onto the ceiling, it didn't sound like the venue would go for it. They weren't sure they had the staff, and the sound tech was hesitant about four people vaulting into the air above his equipment. Minor obstacles, easily overcome at the end of a project that presented one obstacle after another.

60 feet.

Back on the ground, the nervous bandmate had said, "This is a terrible idea." Seconds later, a smiling staff member came over, clipped in our harnesses and said, "This is a great idea!"

70 feet.

The motor stopped. The singer had to climb up onto the edge of the basket to extract himself because the door wouldn't open inward. He yelled and leapt into the void like Superman, swinging a dramatic arc over the crowd.

My turn.

I looked down. Tiny specs of light representing hundreds of people wearing LEDs and glowing face paint were cheering. There I was, with my three best friends, about to play the show of our lives. All those years making music in a rehearsal

Illustration 1   The campaign trail can bring you to some interesting places

room together, all those campaigns created in an office alone, everything brought us to this moment.

I clicked on the power to my goggles and they lit up with every color of the spectrum. I climbed onto the ledge and without a moment's hesitation, jumped into the black. When I felt the ropes engage, after "Don't swing into the first guy," the next thought to run through my head was, "Look where work has taken me today."

NOTE

1 Boston University Dean of Students Kenn Elmore at a PRSSA reception at his home on February 21, 2020.

INVENTION IN PR

"You're better off showing that you aren't just an order taker as early as possible."

– *Chris McMurry, PR pro*[1]

Picture a conveyor belt. At one end of the belt are the product people. They come up with a company's offerings. At the other end of the belt are the communications people. They promote those offerings.

But what if the stuff rolling down the belt sucks? Or what if it's just ok, but it won't set the world on fire?

PR lives or dies on the success or failure of the products and services it rarely has a hand in creating. Many talented communications professionals spend their entire careers at one end of the conveyor belt, waiting to see what a company

DOI: 10.4324/9781003216872-1

drops into their laps. Then they kick into gear, often with the task of turning lemons into lemonade. Sometimes they do it brilliantly.

PR is a creative profession, and its practitioners go to great lengths thinking up ways to generate awareness for brands. But there's a difference between "creative" PR and "Creative PR."

Invention is the difference.

On the one hand, "creative" PR comes up with ideas to promote a product. On the other, "Creative PR" – or what we're calling "Inventive PR" – comes up with great products that almost promote themselves.

After a lifetime of asking clients the usual launch questions ("What's your next product? Who's it for? When's it coming out?") – we started thinking about going at it from a different angle. Maybe we'd start by saying to them, "Here's what your next product might be."

Hold up. Put the PR people in charge of the products? Are you crazy?

Why not? It's happening, and it works.

Across three years and as many industries, my shop launched a trio of campaigns which didn't just put PR in the driver's seat for idea creation; it put PR in charge of product development. The campaigns in our "Invention in PR Trilogy"[2] became the most impactful set of work we'd ever done. We became the only firm committed to an Invention-first approach to PR. Other teams might stumble into it. We would intentionally specialize in it. Once we nailed it down, we shared the secret sauce and encouraged others to do it too.

Invention in PR means coming up with a compelling product or service, conceptualized and filtered through the lens of a PR professional. It uses the same knowledge, skills and abilities PR pros have always applied to building campaigns, while going deeper and channeling everything into the physical or digital object PR eventually promotes.

It doesn't need to be a tangible product. It can be a digital one. It doesn't even need to be a purchasable product. It can be a conceptual one.

Invention creates something out of thin air which didn't previously exist, and drives the campaign. It's not the promotion associated with PR. It's the product and service development associated with R&D. What makes it so powerful is that it's not storytelling. It's storymaking.

Katie Couric said the most important job in journalism isn't telling people what happened; it's getting them to understand why they should care.[3] I like to say PR at its best makes something happen worth caring about.

An Invention-first approach is both the most audacious application or PR, and the most practical. The generation before us fought for and earned a place for PR at the management table. We can express our gratitude by inventing a new table.

And we need to. Consumer brands are bypassing PR firms and looking to their "creative partners" for their biggest campaigns. Marketing executives say they'll entertain a great idea from any discipline (Adweek).[4] Luminaries emphasize idea creation above tools or technology. Marketing legend John Hegarty said, "It will be those people who are best able to come up with ideas and deploy them who will change the future of brands."[5] Unfortunately, PR isn't delivering ideas like it could. Research shows "creative thinking and new

deas" suffered a 17% drop among CMOs as the greatest
benefit of working with a PR agency (PRovoke).[6] Industry
editors highlight "the continued frustration for PR firms"
as they lose their own category in competitions like Cannes,
where recently only a single winning entry in the PR Lions
credited a PR agency with Idea Creation (PRWeek).[7]

Starting down this path begins by asking, "What can this
brand invent or transform which would be interesting?" Or
more simply, "What can we make?"

If it sounds like reverse-engineering PR, it is. If it sounds like
cheating, it is. Ethics exist but rules do not. In the absence of
rules, the greatest sin is to be boring.

Whatever you do, just don't call it "innovation." That word
has become watered down to nothingness, and isn't what
we're talking about.

Innovation streamlines the arrow. Invention creates the bullet.

NOTES

Chris McMurry from MGH in an email to Adam Ritchie (June
26, 2019).

Adam Ritchie Brand Direction. "The Invention in PR Trilogy"
(YouTube). http://youtube.com/playlist?list=PLccCB1oobHKRFvDIxn
BWz4cxbxV-LsqT4

I heard Katie say this when she was interviewed years ago, before
I was in the habit of jotting down the date and venue for words of
wisdom, which I started doing more recently.

Smiley, Minda. "New Study Says In-Housing and Consolidation
Will Further Impact Agencies in 2020" (Adweek, February 21,
2020). http://adweek.com/agencies/new-study-says-in-housing-and-
consolidation-will-further-impact-agencies-in-2020/

Illustration 2 Reese's "Candy Converter" turned unwanted Halloween
candy into Reese's Peanut Butter Cups

5 Hegarty, John. *Hegarty on Advertising* (Thames Hudson, 2011).

6 "Insights: Budgets, Teams & Agencies" (PRovoke, 2020) http://provokemedia.com/ranking-and-data/influence-100/the-influence-100/2020/insights-teams-budgets-agencies

7 Barrett, Steve. "PR Lions: fewer entries, only six Golds and little for PR to celebrate" (PRWeek, June 19, 2020). http://prweek.com/article/1588195/pr-lions-fewer-entries-six-golds-little-pr-celebrate

TYPES AND QUALITY

"Things that are imaginary are important. All we have to do is agree on them being real, and they become real."

— *Neil Gaiman, Author*[1]

TYPES

Every day, I see examples of Invention in PR. Like any passion, when your antenna is up, you begin noticing it wherever you go. Eventually you mentally organize them by their shared characteristics to make sense of it all.

From years of paying attention, I've grouped them into three types:

Type 1: Invention
Inventing a new category of product or service which never existed before, with newsworthiness built into it.

DOI: 10.4324/9781003216872-2

Type 2: Creation
Creating a type of product or service which did exist before, but with a unique story baked into this version.

Type 3: Transformation
Transforming something everyday into something extraordinary, as an avatar or promotional vehicle for the brand.

Some campaigns are purely Type 1 or Type 2. Type 3 can be an overlay. If the Invention transforms something into something else, it's a hybrid.

Type 1 is the rarest to find, the most challenging to pull off and also the hardest to understand. If "new category" is difficult to wrap your head around, just think of Type 1 in terms of function. Type 1s are functionally different than products and services which came before. They *do something* different.

Think of Type 1 as a newsworthy function, Type 2 as a newsworthy creation and Type 3 as a newsworthy transformation.

QUALITY

This is subjective, but helps us aim high when we're dreaming up something new.

We ask if the Invention will be real, or if it will be purely conceptual. Will it be a physical object/functional service, or will it be a digital rendering/lighthearted joke? Then we give them an R or C label for "Real" or "Conceptual." Being Conceptional doesn't make them lesser. Some of the

---

Illustration 3   Three Types of Invention in PR

most effective Inventions in PR make headlines without ever needing to reach tangible form.

Then we ask if it solves a larger problem. Does it have a reason for existing beyond a brand exercise, or does it simply communicate a brand message and demonstrate the brand's personality? We give these a U or F label for "Useful" or "Frivolous." This is where the power of symbolism comes into play, even for the Conceptual.

For example, a new category of product which helps people with a specific medical condition would be a Type 1RU (Real, Useful). A sunscreen which smells like fried chicken put out by a fast-food chain would be a Type 2RF (Real, Frivolous).

Just because something is frivolous doesn't mean it isn't worth doing. You could also think of the F as, "Just for Fun." A computer rendering of a virtual bar spanning a contested international border to prevent the construction of a wall would be a Type 2CU (Conceptual, Useful). Turning bus shelter benches into chair lifts to promote ski tourism would be a Type 3RF (Real, Frivolous), while turning gondola cars into private outdoor dining rooms to help restaurants endure a pandemic would be a Type 3RU (Real, Useful).

All of these examples happened.

Some Inventions in PR are derided by cynics as "PR products."[2] Every year on April Fool's Day, brands release outrageous fake products like "V by Velveeta," a made-up line of luxury skincare products for your skin's "natural, creamy complexion." They earn media and get people talking about the brand, but nobody asked for them and few people would actually purchase and use these products.

The way around skepticism is by making your Inventions useful. By making them answer a need or address a problem. The best of them go further than "because we ould." We're not talking about the social or environmental issues associated with Cause Marketing.[3] Purpose doesn't always have to mean Progressive. It just means having a reason. It's what separates the impactful Inventions from the inconsequential Inventions: the compelling ideas from the gags. Great brand Inventions can wear humor on their sleeves, but when you dig deeper, they're no joke. They have substance because they fix something, or at least symbolize something larger than themselves. They have a 'Why' that's bigger than "to generate media attention." Attention is the initial driver in an Invention in PR, but when you push your Inventions one lever further and find the larger 'Why,' you've really grasped the approach.

LEGO is a brand that's mastered all three types of Inventions in PR. Their Type 1 was "LEGO Braille Bricks," which had bumps and activities to teach children how to read and write Braille, and brought blind and sighted kids together. It was a Type 1 because the product itself did something new. It featured a *newsworthy function*. Their Type 2 was their "Everyone is Awesome" special LGBTQ set, inspired by the Pride flag and featuring 11 monochrome LEGO people, each with their own style and flare, ahead of Pride Month. It was a Type 2 because while the product didn't do anything new, it was a version of a product with news built into it. It was a *newsworthy edition*. Their Type 3 was another Pride Month project: "The World's Smallest Pride Parade." They turned their Westchester, New York MINILAND recreation of New York City into a tiny "parade" of bedazzled LEGO people celebrating the 50th anniversary of the Stonewall Uprising and the birth of the Gay Pride movement. It was a double Type 3 because first they transformed a pile of LEGOs into Times Square, then they transformed their mini Times Square into the site of a commemorative parade. It was a *newsworthy adaptation*.

In the case studies that follow, we'll deconstruct these three main types and show what makes each of them tick.

NOTES

1 Neil Gaiman on looking at the earth from space, versus looking at the borders of countries. I don't remember where I heard him say this. It could have been an audio interview. But it's in line with his comments in an interview with Book Riot on September 17, 2013 and an interview with The Book Slut in October 2006.

2 For a while, I struggled with calling them "PR Inventions." There's baggage associated with that term. And "brand invention" is too close to being just a regular product. That's what brands do: make products. A "branding product" would be closer, but it's too close to "product branding" which is its own field. A "news product" gets confusing because it sounds like news media itself: websites, magazines, etc. A "special edition" sells them short because it doesn't factor earned media into the motive. "Invention PR" sounds like it's PR for an invention, which implies someone else invented it. "Inventive PR" comes closer, but "inventive" gets confused with "creative" more often than it should. I'm coming around to the idea of taking pride in a PR Invention, while still using it sparingly. If nothing else, it means someone listened to a PR person and put resources behind an unusual idea, which is never a bad thing. I also struggled with calling it "Invention in PR," because "Invention PR" would be tighter. But it sounds like you're doing PR for an invention, not also creating one. Even "Cause Marketing" sounds like you're marketing a cause, not necessarily coming up with the cause.

3 Beyond products and services, organizations also have the ability to invent a movement out of thin air. They don't have to be for a serious affliction. Most of those are obvious and taken. They can be a rallying cry for a beloved cultural institution, like Campbell's "Save the Snow Day," which advocated for the preservation of snow days when they disappeared during widespread remote schooling. Or the "10,000 Steps a Day" movement created by Japan's Yamasa Corporation to promote its pedometer in the 1960s. Just like inventing a new product or service, for the invention of a movement, ask yourself, "What's the torch we want this brand to carry?" Then go build the torch. Those movements fall into Types 1, 2 and 3 as well – especially if you're creating a whole new one, putting a new spin on an existing one or transforming one entirely. Resist the urge to slap the brand name onto it if you want widespread adoption. Go back and claim it after it's caught on. Examples of the invention of a movement could fill their own book, beginning with many Edward Bernays and Doris Fleischman campaigns.

TYPE I
INVENTION

"Marketing is the final extension of your art."

– Derek Sivers, Musician[1]

An Invention in PR Type 1 is pure Invention. This is as good as it gets. Beyond just a new product, a Type 1 means you're coming up with a whole new product category which never existed before.

That's what happened with "T.R.I.P.," the world's first album on a beer can.

T.R.I.P. (TYPE 1RU)

Remember the band from the prologue?

DOI: 10.4324/9781003216872-3

Calling The Lights Out just a band sells it short. It's a gang. It's a vehicle for creative freedom, just like the right business can be. Beyond the music, The Lights Out functions like an agency team. The drummer is a designer and creates the artwork. The bass player is a salesman and books the gigs. The singer is a painter and drives his painting van with the band and gear to the shows. I'm the guitarist who comes up with the campaigns.

For our first album, "Color Machine," we worked with a pizza chain to create a meaty Lights Out slice. For our "Rock Pony" EP, we created an online dating profile for the sexy centauress on the cover. For our "Primetime" LP, we sold our storied band van on Craigslist. For our "On Fire" LP, we pegged the recording sessions to a transformer fire which caused a citywide blackout.

After performing at South by Southwest, we went underground and spent three years writing and recording our fourth album. Our singer had a vision about becoming a band that could travel through parallel worlds, and we made a sci-fi record where each song was a report back from across the multiverse. Conceptually out there, sonically accessible. We knew it was our high-water mark, and the tracks were burning holes in our pockets. We were already anxious about the prospect of few people hearing it. Nobody was buying CDs anymore, and a high-cost/low-volume vinyl run wasn't an option. Hundreds of albums were being released every day by independent bands like ours. Even major label acts felt locked in a struggle with obscurity when releasing new material. U2 was sneaking its new album onto unsuspecting smartphones for a shot at awareness. There was too much content. Too few curators. Too little time. No major channels.

I chatted with other musicians at parties, backyard barbecues and clubs during the 20-minute changeover between sets. When I asked them how they found their new music, most said they were going online, where fresh indie albums get lost like needles in the world's largest haystack. They weren't visiting record stores like they once did. Those stores were stocking more Hello Kitty and Star Wars merchandise than music, just to stay alive. If the stores carried new music inventory, it wasn't from unsigned indies; they were selling vinyl reissues from legacy acts and the already-famous. But when I talked to these musicians about how often they went into a craft beer or wine store, they were regulars. Craft beer was at the peak of its second boom. The beer industry looked like it was growing as quickly as the music industry was shrinking. Craft beer labels were getting the same artistic love and attention as the intricate vinyl album covers of the classic rock era.

At this point in my life, I'd done enough beer PR to know most craft beer drinkers make their decisions at the point of sale, and how influential packaging can be. And I'd done enough music PR to know the value of a CD from an unsigned act was less than zero. Context makes the sale, and unless you're selling it immediately following a show where the band just blew a roomful of minds, you couldn't give those plastic discs away with a gun.

One day at our rehearsal space in a break between songs, I said it would be cool if we released this album on cans of craft beer. The guys were curious and a little skeptical of how it might work. I said if people weren't going to discover the album in a music store or online, and weren't going to pay for it even if they did – why wouldn't we put it somewhere we knew they'd find it, on a product they were already paying a premium price for, and make news as the first group in history to do it. Why not release this album on a beer?

Easier said than done. For months I shopped the idea to breweries and got nowhere. Rejection or radio silence. I kept asking my bandmates for a little more time until we felt like we'd exhausted every option.

I shared my frustration with my friend Nate from the band Scamper. Instead of shrugging (Nate's picture is on the Wikipedia entry for the word, "shrug."[2] For real, check it out.), he asked if we'd approached Aeronaut Brewing Co. – a brewery founded by scientists from Cornell and MIT.

I got home, reached out to their general company email address and heard back the next night from their co-founder, Ben, who invited me to the brewery for a meeting. We took a walk around the block. He told me about their art-meets-science culture and beers that tell a story. I told him we had an album about parallel realities. He asked, "Oh, you mean like the multiverse?" In that moment, I knew we'd come to the right place. I mentioned what I also did for a living and committed to promoting the collaboration. He said, "That's all good, but I'm really excited about releasing your album on our beer." Just like that, the pressure was off. But not really. I was still going to work this thing like mad. And he still had to come up with a beer.

I walked out of that meeting thinking, "Holy shit, this could actually happen." Finding an Invention partner is like dating. You ask people out, run the gamut of disconnection to false starts and complain to your friends, "Dating is so hard." Then you find someone who sticks and think, "I didn't know it could be this easy."

Ben brought the challenge to his team and the idea "spread like wildfire." They went at it like a science project. The beer would fuel a pandimensional traveler's journey between universes, and the music would be the soundtrack to that journey. When they asked us, "What kind of beer do you want?" We said, "You didn't tell us what kind of album to make, so we're not going to tell you what kind of beer to brew. Just listen to the rough cut of the album and brew whatever it inspires." They were so into it, they even used Galaxy hops from the other side of the world in the recipe. It was an "imperial session" IPA. Which if you know beer, is paradox. Imperial means high alcohol. Session means all-night easy drinking. But if you believe the universe is infinite, then paradoxes must exist somewhere out there.

We trusted each other to get it right. The album could have sounded awful, but they were committed. The beer could have tasted awful, but we were committed. Thank God they were both good. And that they were both finished in time, because they almost weren't.

Packaging was critical. In one meeting between the band and the brewers, Ben and I were sitting at a table with Raul, the brewery's label artist who also illustrates SpongeBob SquarePants comics. We gave Raul photos and videos of the band wearing its synchronized light gear and talked to him about the concept. (Synchronized light gear? Oh yes. For this album, our drummer covered us in 1,000 individually-assigned LEDs, shining across our bodies and instruments in time with the music. We called it the Color Machine and it became the vehicle that transported the band and its audience through the darkness between realities.) In the amount of time it took to drink a beer, Raul sketched his first draft of the label. It was perfect. There was a pandimensional traveler, a machine flying through a wormhole and an all-seeing eye. Every visual element was pulled from the album.

Next, we had to figure out how to trigger the content. After mixed results experimenting with a Twitter service which functioned like an auto-responder, I was in New York City for a client event. I stopped into Hellcat Annie's Tap Room for a beer, and a bearded guy sat next to me and ordered a Heady Topper. You don't often see that brew outside of Vermont, so I cheers'd him on his good taste. His name was Kyle and he was a coder. I asked him if it would be possible to install a script on a Twitter account which would listen for a hashtag and send a tweet to that person, with copy pulled from a database. Kyle said, "I could code that in an hour."

We designed a social media trigger onto the label and installed Kyle's script on the band's Twitter account, making it an album-dispensing digital fortune cookie. Every time #TRIPME (like "beer me") was posted by a consumer, they'd receive a message back from the band, telling them what they were doing right now in a parallel universe, and giving them a link to the album's landing page. The band wrote and uploaded reponses like, "In a parallel universe, you're a master artist who only paints iPhones: thelightsout.com/trip," "In a parallel universe, the asteroid missed, the dinosaurs survived, and you're riding a pterodactyl to work: thelightsout.com/trip" and "In a parallel universe, you're candlepin bowling with Queen Elizabeth: thelightsout.com/trip." Consumers could drink, listen and chat with the band all at once. Putting a download code on the cans would have been easier. But we wanted to make the process fun and interactive.

We called the whole project, "T.R.I.P.," short for "The Reckonings in Pandimensionality." This hybrid digital/physical item would be a new way for consumers to experience music, with full sensory immersion in sound, taste, touch, visual and smell.

Our expense budget was $1,000. Remember this was just four dudes funding it out of their own pockets, after already spending most of their money on studio time.

This was all before the product was ready. What most people view as PR hadn't even started yet. With the Invention approach, the Invention comes first. Invention in PR means forging the silver bullet you need to run a campaign.

When you're working on a product with an in-depth backstory, you need a launch video[3] explaining it. The band

---

Illustration 4   "T.R.I.P.," the world's first album on a beer can from The Lights Out and Aeronaut Brewing Co.

went to the brewery with our longtime video collaborator Leesa. One problem: the beer can label prints weren't ready yet. Ben drove an hour outside the city to pick up a batch of test labels from the printer so we could complete the shoot. Then he gave an on-camera interview despite nearly losing his voice to a bug. Ben was a hero that day. The band watched our album being packaged and tasted the final product. The feeling of seeing this go from idea, to pitch, to running off the assembly line in a real life product was indescribable. Row after row of cans were stacked on top of each other. I climbed up a mountain of them. It was one of the happiest days of my life.

We brought in Ulf Oesterle, the chair of the music industry program at Syracuse University as our music industry expert, and Ben Hogue from Berklee College of Music, who teaches a course on music and food pairings as our food expert. For the media outreach, we untethered ourselves from the usual suspects. Angles were tailored for food, beverage, beer, pop culture, lifestyle, business, technology, design, science, packaging and visual arts outlets.

My friend Abby was the event manager for a climbing gym, which happened to be located next to the brewery. After being wow'd by our wearable light show, she asked us about playing a party there. We decided to make the climbing gym performance the launch event for both the album and the beer. Just like that, we had an event manager for free. It was Abby's job to organize great events for the venue. By working our release, she was just doing her job. Not only would Abby do the planning, but she'd manage the sound, lighting, stage, safety crews and liquor license. Those things would have been the straws that broke our backs if we had to take care of them on top of everything else. Thank you, Abby.

It was going to be a tough launch. We were planning it for the stretch of time between Thanksgiving and Christmas: not the best window to roll out a new story. But when beer is ready, it needs to move out the door. Everything was coming together as we headed into release week, which happened to also be the week of the 2016 presidential election. We thought it would be a one- or two-day news story. We were wrong.

That election ended up dominating the news cycle for four years. When it first hit, our target audience didn't care about a fun beer album. They were fending off panic attacks. We were staring down the noisiest, densest, most challenging launch climate we'd ever seen.

When we announced the project, you could hear crickets. It was demoralizing. If you've ever felt like you were assigned an impossible product to promote, try working a self-released album from an unsigned rock band. And that's in normal times. For this one, even though I thought we created something that would punch through the sound barrier, suddenly it felt like we'd never achieve liftoff. I thought I wasn't as good a musician and I hoped to be. I thought I wasn't as good a PR person as I hoped to be. All of my self-worth was riding on this and I couldn't let the patient die on the operating table.

I was back in New York for an event when the first story hit.[4] It wasn't even one I pitched. It unbelievably came from the press release,[5] days later. I was over the moon. We'd achieved that coveted national piece of entertainment coverage. We'd punched through the atmosphere. When another outlet picked up the story, it put the band alongside Beyoncé and Taylor Swift in terms of creative album dropping.[6]

Now I could go about the work knowing that we'd already reached a main objective. Now it was about seeing how far we could take it.

We came up with a series of touchpoints, and needed all of them. Every few weeks, we released a new track, a music video[7] with a media partner, announced another show or added some other new element to keep the story going. The needle had to be threaded through the election, Thanksgiving, the religious holidays, Inauguration Day, the Women's March, the Travel Ban and then Super Bowl Sunday. (At least that one gave us an opening to talk about beer!)

We even shifted our outreach to the UK when things got too politically charged at home. It felt like flying an airplane around a weather system. We positioned the product as perfect for consumers "who feel like they just woke up in an alternate reality." Even National Beer Can Appreciation Day was used as an angle to shift attention back to beer when all anyone wanted to talk about was politics.

We got a second crack at it that summer when a second batch was brewed. You'd think it would have gone smoother, but nothing is ever easy. A redesign in Aeronaut's beer label template caused the social media trigger to be accidentally dropped. The brewery fixed it by putting stickers with the social info on every set of cans to go out the door. We turned the canning day into a media event.[8] As PR pros, we prep clients for on-camera interviews all the time. We know it's hard, but we don't appreciate how hard until we're in the interview hot seat ourselves. It gave me a whole new perspective on what we put our clients through.

A funny thing happened on the second canning day. My account coordinator and I drove fresh samples of the album to the city's NPR affiliate. We didn't have an appointment. The arts editor hadn't responded to our heads-up that we were coming, so I was going to talk my way past the front desk and into her office. I wasn't sure how, but when all else fails, you improvise. The receptionist challenged us right away. I told him we were there to hand-deliver a fresh sample of a sci-fi inspired album, packaged in a way the editor had never seen before. The receptionist said he was a musician and described an unforgettable show he'd recently seen by a group called The Lights Out, which claimed to come from a parallel universe. I smiled, looked at his name badge and said, "Nathaniel, that was my band, and this is our new record." He grabbed the phone, called the arts editor and told her she needed to get down to reception immediately. The AC looked stunned, and the feature aired a few weeks later.[9]

For everyone else, we sent the beer samples in pint-sized tubes. Why tubes? Not only because they already had the shape of a can. If you're a busy editor with square boxes and padded envelopes piled up on your desk every day, which package would you reach for first: the same old box or the cool cylinder? I won't go into how we got them to these editors. If you're not breaking some rules, it's not a good PR campaign.

For the second release show, we made the live production even bigger. More beer, more lights, more lasers. Always more lasers. Once again, the band's wearable light show made jaws drop and phones rise. If you've ever attended a show in a rock club, half the audience is looking at their phones. The challenge for the performer is: can you make something happen on stage that's more compelling than whatever's happening on someone's social feed? I call it the 90 Degree Rule. Can you make them turn their phones from horizontal to the ground (—) to perpendicular to the ground (|), pointed at the stage to capture what's happening there? If you can do that, you're winning.

I spent every available hour pitching this story. It was a fight every step of the way, but yielded MarketWatch,[10] NPR, Adweek,[11] UPROXX, Paste Magazine,[12] Food & Wine,[13] Men's Journal,[14] The A.V. Club[15] and more – reactively earning coverage as far away as Russia, Finland and Thailand. When we used Google Translate on the articles abroad, we were happy to see they all got the facts right. Which was nice, because it would have been a little awkward to chase down a correction in Russia at a time when the

U.S. was confronting it over election meddling. We hit more than 106.9 million press impressions and 13.7 million social impressions.

Half of those stories had to be pulled out of the fire because the editor who was initially interested got a new job, or the writer who'd interviewed us left the outlet before submitting the story. Every story that made it was a small miracle. Just when you think something's in the bag, forces beyond your control conspire to derail it.

At a certain point, we could feel it catching on. Mid-campaign, when I was working the story so hard smoke was pouring from my laptop's USB ports, an old friend from college reached out to me and said, "I'm sitting at a bar in Maine and two people next to me are talking about your beer can album." You can't beat that. If you ever want to make a PR person's day, tell them you saw their work in the wild.

It was important that this wasn't seen as just a PR stunt. Remember the Types of Invention in PR? You want it to be Useful, not Frivolous. We ticked that box with messaging that we were trying to reintroduce the immersive "quest" aspect to new music discovery which vanished in the digital age. This was a viable way to release new music and we succeeded in getting that message across. ("How the beer aisle suddenly became a record store" – MarketWatch) ("A novel direction" – NPR) ("Unconventional ingenuity" – The A.V. Club) ("A new high in album dropping" –UPROXX).

Competing releases from established artists, without a food/beverage component, suddenly appeared flat. Even other beers from major label artists which came out that same month(!) didn't have the new music social distribution component. They looked like yellow liquid with a label slapped onto it.

Most importantly, people liked it. They ran to beer stores and posted images of themselves hoisting the world's first beer can album into the air, and posted the social media trigger to get the music. The same people who would never have purchased or streamed the album were putting on their shoes, going to a store, buying it and sharing their excitement over social media. The day I walked into a beer store and saw people buying it off the shelf was another one of the best days of my life.

There was humor. When you give someone a beer at 7.5% ABV and instructions to tap into their phone, they don't always get it right on the first try. One person who may have had too many T.R.I.P.s took several tries to craft the tweet.

There was drama. The brand manager from another brewery tweeted something negative about the idea to a national beer industry reporter. The reporter defended our concept. The brewery's CEO got involved and used the F word at the reporter. The reporter told them, "This is the wrong hill for either of you to die on." Beer lovers snacked on virtual popcorn as they watched another brewery destroy its relationship with one of the most influential writers in their category.

There was lawlessness. After getting our Twitter account verified, we got it suspended. It turns out you're not allowed to install automated scripts that bot'ify your account. We knew this might pose a problem, but took the calculated risk. Remember, if you're not breaking some rules, it's not a good campaign. By the time Twitter caught on, the campaign was mostly over, and we earned back our access after it won a national marketing award for Best Use of Twitter.

There was even a little thievery. A few months later, a major brewery used copy about the relationship between beer and music that was eerily similar to "T.R.I.P."'s press release, in its own press announcement about a collaboration beer with a major artist. Back in Boston, another brewery began releasing special edition beers with local bands. This was fine by us. We even bylined a story in a music industry trade teaching other bands how to do it![16] The only disappointing part was none of them were using the beer to release new music. If you're going to borrow an idea, at least match it or top it with your own unique take on it. Don't go halfway.

In the end, we sold nearly 6,000 beer can albums. One way to gauge the success of an Invention in PR is by asking, "Did it sell?" This one sold out. Twice. We wanted one national piece of coverage and ended up with 70. Our pre-release social engagement was flat, and we boosted it to reach millions of listeners through social over the course of the year. We went from playing tiny clubs with indie bands to playing boat cruises with major national acts, to big theaters opening up for our heroes.

We started out backed into the corner of a seemingly unsolvable communications challenge: getting consumers to engage with a new album from an unknown, unsigned band. To answer it, we developed a new way to distribute music. It felt like we made a historic dent in a fiercely competitive market. "T.R.I.P." was an answer to a problem plaguing the music industry for decades, put physical discovery back on the table for music consumers longing for a more tangible relationship with their music and used technology to solve a problem technology initially created.

Not bad for a thousand bucks, or the cost of 10 cases of beer. The band even earned money on the launch events because it sold tickets to them. How often does a product launch event become a revenue stream instead of a cost center? Not often. Use your network.

Accomplishing a lot with a little is very PR. There were no celebrity spokespeople or exorbitant spends. Just an original idea and the effort to make it real. The label of the beer began with the words, "This beer is an experiment...." The experiment worked.[17]

"T.R.I.P." went on to win every award in the industry, including more PRSA Silver Anvil Awards than any campaign in the country. Ben, Leesa and I attended fancy dinners where elegantly dressed attendees went from wondering, "Who are those guys?" to "Them again?!" I got misty-eyed walking down the same street I'd walked to pitch Aeronaut in that first meeting, this time to drop off a trophy reaffirming their leap of faith in the project.

We even got to do it again a few years later for our next album, "Night Vision," which we released using Spotify Codes[18] printed on the label of a black IPA bearing the record's name. After turning the beer aisle into a record store, we turned a brewery into a record label.

When I started working on "T.R.I.P.," my PR shop was up against the ropes, down to its last client. A lot of business-minded people would tell you to start dialing for dollars and to put all of your effort into winning new clients like your life depended on it. Instead, I went all in on a campaign for no money and it became the defining moment of my career. I knew there would always be new clients. And eventually there were.

Sometimes you're trying to write your "Bohemian Rhapsody," and it turns out you're writing your "Fellowship of the Ring." More on that in the next two chapters.

If you're speeding through this book, this is the most detailed case study because it was a labor of love which lasted years. The ones that came after were quicker hits.

MY SPECIAL AFLAC DUCK (TYPE 1RU)

As I was finishing the "T.R.I.P." campaign, I reconnected with my mentor, Carol Cone. She founded the first social impact agency in the country, which was the first place I worked after college. Carol told me about an idea she was developing for Aflac: bringing its famous mascot to life, in the form of an interactive social robot, which would be a comforting companion for children undergoing an average of 1,000 days of cancer treatments.

The project was called "My Special Aflac Duck"[19] and it had just taken CES, the country's biggest consumer electronics show, by storm. It was the one product at CES you couldn't buy, because Aflac was pledging to donate thousands of them to every child with cancer in the U.S. who wanted one.

Carol makes connections. She finds unlikely collaborators, puts them together and breaks through. Her idea for "My Special Aflac Duck" was cooked up over lunch. Her colleague, Aaron, was telling her about the social robots he was making to help children face critical illnesses. Carol had just started working with Aflac. "Suddenly there was a huge thunderclap in my brain, where Aaron's social robot creations collided with the Aflac duck," she said. "I had a huge smile and shouted to Aaron, 'We're going to create a social robot duck for Aflac!'" Eighteen months later, they'd captured the hearts of children across the country. Soon after, they won a place in TIME Magazine's Best Inventions of the Year.

Imagine that. A product conceived by a PR pro being recognized as one of the greatest inventions in the world. It's possible. It happened. It was one of the most lauded and impactful programs of its time.

Illustration 5 "My Special Aflac Duck" brought a mascot to life for pediatric cancer patients

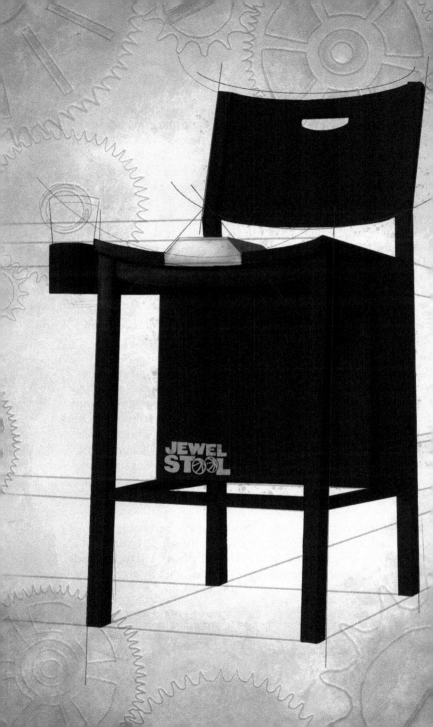

Both "T.R.I.P." and "My Special Aflac Duck" are a hybrid of Type 1 and Type 3. They both created new product categories, and there was a transformation involved. We turned an album into a beer. Carol turned a mascot into an animatron.

OTHERS

As we look at other examples, many of them weren't created by PR teams. They were thought up by other disciplines. They could and should have been created by PR teams because they were clearly designed to earn media just by existing. That's what puts them in the PR wheelhouse, and why PR pros should take note. Some people call them "brand inventions," and they are. But that takes the 'why' out of it. The 'why' is 'earned media.' And that's the homeland – if no longer the sole property – of PR.

What makes them a Type 1? They do something no previous product or service has done.

- "The Home that Runs on Dunkin" was a mobile hotel which ran on spent Dunkin' coffee grounds. You could rent and live in it.
- "LifeFaker.com" was a spoof online service for people to fake their perfect influencer lives. It came with digital assets like photos of reflecting pools. Its creator, the mental health nonprofit Sanctus, wanted to spark a conversation about the negative consequences of influencer culture. (You gotta love anything that takes the piss out of privileged influencer culture, and we'll get into that later as well.)
- "The Oreo Music Box" was a record player, reinvented to play a cookie. It tapped into cool tech, the vinyl record craze and childhood nostalgia cleverly timed for holiday gift-giving.

Illustration 6   "The Jewel Stool" from Buffalo Wild Wings helped newly vasectomized men enjoy March Madness in comfort

- "The Nivea Sunslide" was a special waterslide designed to coat up to 100 kids per hour in SPF 50+ waterproof sunscreen at the beach, making an otherwise annoying process fun.
- "The Will You? Ring" by Carmichael Lynch Relate for Helzberg Diamonds was a plain silver band which said, "This is a ring, not the ring." They invented it to help someone propose, get the "yes" and then shop for the actual engagement ring with their partner.
- "The Jewel Stool" came from Buffalo Wild Wings, when data showed more men scheduled vasectomies around March Madness than any other time of the year. They turned this insight into a special chair which cooled your balls and your beer at the same time.
- "The Coors Light" smart beer tap lit up whenever Budweiser's social media platforms posted something negative about Coors. This was Jiu Jitsu-level Invention in PR because it took an opponent's negative energy and turned it against them.

All of these Inventions did something completely new. They didn't fit into a category, and they defined their own.

NOTES

1 Sivers, Derek. *Your Music and People* (Hit Media, 2020).

2 Wikipedia. "Shrug" http://en.wikipedia.org/wiki/Shrug

3 "The Lights Out + Aeronaut: T.R.I.P. Album + Beer Trailer" (YouTube). http://youtu.be/uG4_4G-_FH4

4 Johnson, Zach. "This Band Just Dropped Their Latest Album Via A Craft Beer Can" (UPROXX, November 3, 2016). http://uproxx.com/life/craft-beer-music-album-release/

5 The Lights Out. "Band and Brewery Release an Album on a Beer Can" (PRWeb, November 1, 2016). http://prweb.com/releases/2016/10/prweb13808727.htm

6 Lauterbach, David. "Band to release new album via beer can, which is a very 2016 sentence" (The Comeback, November 6, 2016). http://thecomeback.com/pop-culture/band-to-release-new-album-via-beer-can-which-is-a-very-2016-sentence.html

7 The Lights Out. "'Waves of Sound' (Official)" (YouTube). http://youtu.be/W7JQN8UjQP8

8 The Lights Out. "TLO on NBC" (YouTube). http://youtu.be/FXIGpQN6Ud4

9 Shea, Andrea. "Boston Rock Band Releases New Album On A Beer Can" (WBUR, August 1, 2017). http://wbur.org/artery/2017/07/31/music-on-a-beer-can

10 Notte, Jason. "How the beer aisle suddenly became a record store" (MarketWatch, January 27, 2017). http://marketwatch.com/story/how-the-beer-aisle-suddenly-became-a-record-store-2017-01-25

11 Monllos, Christina. "This Band Went to a Brewery to Release Their Album and Created a Beer to Go With It" (Adweek, February 1, 2017). http://adweek.com/creativity/this-band-went-to-a-brewery-to-release-their-album-and-created-a-beer-to-go-with-it/

12 Sandy, Matt. "Brew News: What The Election Results Mean For Beer" (Paste Magazine, November 11, 2016). http://pastemagazine.com/drink/craft-beer-/brew-news-what-the-election-results-mean-for-beer/

13 Pomranz, Mike. "The Year in Canned Beer" (Food & Wine, June 26, 2017). http://foodandwine.com/drinks/beer-can-news-82-anniversary

14 Wolinski, Cat. "Beer is the New Vinyl: Boston-Based Band Releases Album on a Beer Can" (Men's Journal, November 10, 2016). http://mensjournal.com/food-drink/beer-is-the-new-vinyl-boston-based-band-releases-album-on-a-beer-can-w449734/

15 Colburn, Randall. "Boston sci-fi rockers The Lights Out release new album on a pack of beer" (The A.V. Club, November 21, 2016). http://avclub.com/boston-sci-fi-rockers-the-lights-out-release-new-album-1798254565

16 Ritchie, Adam. "How to Partner With Local Breweries on Your Next Album Release" (Performer Magazine, February 20, 2017). http://performermag.com/band-management/music-promotion/how-to-partner-with-local-breweries-on-your-next-album-release/

17 Adam Ritchie Brand Direction. "T.R.I.P. – Campaign Sizzle Reel (Official)" (YouTube). http://youtu.be/5FGzuMWG1Dg

18 Johnson, Theresa Christine. "This Band Released their Album on Spotify … on a Beer Can" (The Dieline, December 18, 2018). http://thedieline.com/blog/2018/12/18/this-band-released-their-album-on-spotifyon-a-beer-can?

19 Freethink. "The Robot Duck Helping Kids With Cancer | Freethink" (YouTube). http://youtu.be/ed5uKLlQKFo

TYPE II
CREATION

"It's like creating magic, isn't it? You can create something from an idea you think up. And then you can bring it to life via a campaign!"
– Patrice Tanaka, PR pro[1]

An Invention in PR Type 2 is creation, or Invention-lite. It's coming up with a product which may not appear different on the surface, but has a newsworthy story built into it from the start. You're not defining a new category or making something functionally different from what came before, but you're making a version of something that's headline-level interesting when you hear the story behind it.

We did this with "Mix It Up," our campaign for a collection of organic cafes.

DOI: 10.4324/9781003216872-4

MIX IT UP (TYPE 2RU)

Adam: *"We're gonna turn influencers into food!"*
Friend: *"That sounds like cannibalism."*
Adam: *"You're right. We'll find another way to describe it."*

I met Jonathan when we both worked on the Perrier account at Cone. One time on a new business pitch, I sent a police officer after him in the restroom of an In-N-Out Burger by LAX. Despite the practical joke, he still wanted to mentor me. Years later, he was leading PR for Panera, and then KIND, the healthy snack company. His former boss at Panera, Ron Shaich, had sold the company and bought an organic cafe brand called Life Alive. Ron's team was looking to put PR behind Life Alive, and Jonathan recommended my shop.

The location Life Alive wanted to promote was new, but it wasn't *brand new*. It had a soft opening in June, and now we were in August. When we soft-sounded media about it, some editors had already taken lunch breaks there. None of them had written about it because nobody asked them to. And now it was old news to them. With new restaurants popping up in the city every day – hundreds each year – the minute you serve your first customer, you're open, whether you call the opening "soft" or "grand."

So how were we going to get the word out about a cool cafe when it was up and running months before we came onboard?

On the press side, we had an ace up our sleeve with Ron. He hadn't yet told his post-Panera story. Our press strategy could use Ron's fast-casual dining expertise by casting Life Alive as the third act in a play which began when he founded Au Bon Pain and Panera. Then we'd break the news of Life Alive's *next* planned location by showcasing the flagship location's look and feel as the shape of things to come.

On the social side, we knew this needed to be an Instagram campaign because the audience was young, active and food-focused. A little poking around told us they equated food with culture and saw it as an expression of who they were. They loved to hear the story behind their food, enjoyed behind-the-scenes prep content and things that came in small batches. Cone recently published research showing 81% of them believed they could have an impact on social issues by using social media.[2]

First, we needed someone who personally knew the right influencers. Enter my mentee, Kate. She was right in the target audience and regularly hung out with the foodies, health nuts and students we were looking to engage.

One day, I was walking on my treadmill desk, and Kate was working next to me.

step, step

As a micro-influencer herself, I asked Kate how she would respond if a cafe brand reached out to her with an offer to create a product in her honor, and named it after her Instagram handle. She liked the idea.

step, step, step

I kept walking and asked, "What if we did this on a larger scale, and brought together a bunch of Instagrammers across food, health and student life, maybe from different backgrounds, asked what they enjoyed eating when they were growing up and created a version of those dishes together with them. Would it be exciting to be part of that?" She said yes.

step, step, step, step

By now I was waving my arms around. "What if a portion of the proceeds from those dishes went to wellness nonprofits, and the influencers got to choose where the money went? What if we offered them an opportunity to use their platforms for good?" She said they'd appreciate that.

step, step, step, step, step

I asked Kate, "What should we call the program? It's got action, variety and experimentation. How about 'Mix It Up?'" She liked the name.[3]

At the time, I was thinking a lot about Joseph Campbell and the hero's journey. A few friends recently introduced me to his books, and I liked the way he uncovered the framework on which most tales have been based for thousands of years, from Jesus to Star Wars. I wondered if we could use one of the oldest storytelling structures known to man, and apply it to digital influencer PR. Maybe we could simplify the hero's journey from its original 12 stages, and make it a quest with four chapters.

Chapter 1 would be "The Call to Adventure": a welcome dinner for the entire group of influencers, where we'd initiate them into the project. Chapter 2 would be "Meeting the Mentor": one-on-one prep sessions in the kitchen with the brand's culinary director. Chapter 3 would be "The Transformation": their social handles turning into signature dishes sold for one week in the cafe. Chapter 4 would be "The Return": their delivery of funds to their chosen nonprofits.

Epic storytelling has always revolved around food. We'd approach this campaign as if we were writing brand mythology, with the influencer as the hero.

Constructing the program this way could create four opportunities for each influencer to willingly post about Life Alive as they moved through their journey: a scenario where millions of targeted social impressions could be sustained across several months on a $0 PR expense budget.

We pitched it to Keith, who managed the Life Alive brand. He said yes, and that was it. We had our campaign.

Now it was time to kick the tires on it.

I asked Kate who among the city's food, health and student Instagram set were the most responsible and responsive. Who went to the same events and panels she went to? Who would she trust to involve with a project and follow it through? Could they be as diverse as the range of people who love Life Alive? Could they have at least a few thousand highly engaged followers who leave real, substantive comments on their posts? Could we inspire a contagious level of emotion among them by treating them like an elite cohort, moving through an experience together and writing an arc which would allow them to be the heroes of their own online stories?

She came up with a list of candidates and reached out to them with an offer to join us, Ron and the brand's culinary director, Leah. Days later, we were sitting in front of them at the cafe. They all showed up! Say what you will about Gen Z'ers. They didn't let us down! Most of them already knew each other, and it was as much a reason for them all to catch up as it was to sample the food, which was fine by us.

It was part focus group, part welcome dinner. It had the feel of an initiation combined with a family reunion as everyone sat around a single table.

We listened to their thoughts on the brand and the new space. We ordered a sample of nearly everything on the menu and saw what caught their attention. Ron talked about the vision for the cafes. The biggest challenge was attempting this in the middle of a dinner rush with a kitchen staff still in training. The food took a little time to come out, and Kate and I were sweating bullets. It was worth the wait. Each dish was given the movie star treatment, with dozens of photos and videos snapped on delivery.

Near the end of the evening, I told the group Life Alive would like to collaborate with them on new menu items, champion them by naming the dishes after their Instagram handles and donate a portion of proceeds to a wellness nonprofit they got to choose. This wasn't just the usual brand hitting them up for a photo promotion. We were saying, "Let's create and do something good at the same time."

They were all onboard.

The one-on-one prep sessions in the months that followed brought each influencer into the kitchen, where we asked them to share flavor memories from their own backgrounds, while Leah set out the ingredients. One made deconstructed tacos to honor her Mexican heritage and said, "They taste like my grandma's frijoles!" Another made Asian peanut noodles to share her memories of home cooking. Another made a Mediterranean-inspired falafel salad to recognize her Greek roots.

These sessions were a blast. We'd catch the subway from the office to the cafe and help document the experience for that week's influencer. We'd interview them about their time in the kitchen with Leah and what the project meant to them. We equipped them with the multimedia content they needed for their second chapter of posts, teasing their individual collaborations.

Emotion would drive the posts, and with no contracts, everything came down to how well we could inspire our influencers to post willingly. One was moved to tears during her prep session. Another told us having her own dish was a dream come true and made her feel like she'd arrived. Another brought his parents, who said how proud they were.

Another said she'd never had the ability to create beyond her photo feed before.

We worked with Life Alive's design firm on point-of-sale materials to promote the unveiling of each dish. We introduced one dish per week over three months, worked with the influencers to alert their followers and celebrated each launch with them, achieving the third chapter of posts. Finally, we invited them to document the delivery of the funds they helped raise, for the fourth chapter.

For press offsite, we ran a series of food drops to bring the Life Alive experience directly to editors. Each drop contained a small taste of the menu and a press kit, hand-delivered by the team.

A funny thing about those media drops. We reached out to editors at every outlet at least a week ahead of time, letting them know we'd be coming by, and almost nobody got back to us. We did our due diligence and followed up, and it was still mostly silence. So, without any appointments, we showed up on their doorstep and talked our way into every newspaper, magazine, business journal, website and radio station that mattered. We made it past every security desk, every reception area and into every office kitchen where Leah and I pitched the editors face-to-face. Meanwhile, Kate sat in Leah's car, which we double parked outside each building. When we left the cafe that morning, Leah asked Kate if she could drive manual. Kate hesitantly said she could. When we were done for the day, Kate confided in me that she didn't know how to drive stick, and misunderstood Leah's question! I asked, "What were you going to do if a cop knocked on the window and asked you to move the car?" She said, "I thought about that, and my plan was to cry!" We both laughed.[4]

Illustration 7 "Mix It Up": Influencer-inspired dishes containing a story from Life Alive

The press we conducted onsite wasn't seat-of-the-pants. We invited national food media to the cafe to tour the space and interview Ron one-on-one about his legendary fast casual experience in the context of Life Alive's expansion. Then we fed the influencer program directly into the press program as a fresh angle, and presented the whole Life Alive story as a well-balanced meal.

Of course, there were setbacks. One editor spent half a day with Ron in the cafe – a generous amount of time from one of the top CEOs in the country – and we thought we had a major feature in the bag. Hours later, she asked for a custom photo of Ron, which we lined up that night. We got her everything she needed, and then she disappeared. No story. No response to follow-up. The client understandably kept asking for updates, and even though it was out of our control it was embarrassing for us.

There were also some lessons learned and applied on etiquette. My mentor, Steve, whose PR agency has repped everyone from Paul McCartney to Foo Fighters, ritually visits a music store on the day his clients release an album, and buys a copy. Even though he has hundreds of press copies on his sample shelf, he always buys one for good luck. When these Life Alive creations came out every week, I thought of Steve and made a point to buy every one with my own money. I was sitting at the counter enjoying one of them, and it was so good, my laptop, phone and reading material were put away. Leah came over, noticed I wasn't doing anything except appreciating the food and said, "Thank you for eating mindfully."[5]

So how did the campaign do?

We tripled the brand's social interactions. The "Mix It Up" dishes were craveworthy, with comments and shares on our cohorts' platforms like, "I Def have to get this! All my fav things" (tastes2totango), "Omg I wanna try this so bad," (lizzzeats) and "@hannah_meiseles we need to go here" (northeastern). On Live Alive's platforms, they drew comments like, "Can we go here @dianabarrie:):):)" (leannkosior), "@smgs219 omg go go go! I'm so jealous" (lilmarissaleigh) and "@rachel_nadolny omg definitely need to get this" (hmonbleau). 15.4 million target consumers were reached through earned social.

We solidified Life Alive's reputation as a top healthy eating destination: "The best healthy restaurants in Boston" (Bon Appétit),[6] "Life Alive is a favorite, and made it their mission to provide you with tons of healthy options" (Fitt Boston)[7] and "Life Alive makes healthy eating delicious, accessible" (BrooklineHub).[8] We used Ron effectively and cemented his reputation as a fast casual authority bringing his extensive expertise to the brand: "Panera founder has quietly launched a fast-casual empire" (Food & Wine)[9] and "Panera and Au Bon Pain founder Ron Shaich is driving Life Alive's next era of expansion" (Eater).[10] The Boston Herald called our "Mix It Up" dishes "recipes from local tastemakers."[11] 31.6 million target consumers were reached through earned press: 31 times the brand's previous period.

Most importantly, we helped contribute to a 6% increase in quarterly sales at the flagship cafe, during a time of year when most of the people in that neighborhood were away on end-of-year holidays.

Beyond the objectives, we gave the brand fodder for more than a third of its owned posts, sold hundreds of special dishes and raised thousands of dollars for wellness nonprofits. Beyond the campaign's lifespan, five of the dishes created during "Mix It Up" became permanent menu options, where they continued helping the company's bottom line.

PR ran the show. It created new products when it needed them. They weren't new product categories; that would have made them a Type 1. But they were a product line with built-in newsworthiness. Along with Keith, Leah, Ron and their partners, we put Life Alive at the center of the city's healthy living, food and student scenes, elevated the brand to the national level, nourished nonprofits and baked an authentic personal story into every digital dish.[12]

When someone sticks their neck out for you and introduces you to a viable client, you want to make good on their vote of confidence. After "Mix It Up" was recognized in every PR competition and came out on top over McDonald's, Baskin-Robbins and Dunkin' as PR Daily's Best Food and Beverage Campaign, I shared the news with Jonathan and thanked him again for thinking of me. If you want to show your appreciation for a referral, go kill it for them.

The funny thing was, I'd never done an Instagram influencer program before. And we still pulled this one off without an expense budget. Neither of those things mattered. Influencers use brands for their own ends, to burnish their own reputations. If you can't offer money, offer prestige. Treat them like individuals and honor their individuality. Give them an opportunity to make something, not just snap a photo. And top it off with a chance to have a positive impact on others. You don't need deep experience with a technology platform to make something work. You need a good idea, an understanding of how humans behave and a great connector on your team – and we had all of them.

HEARTS ON FIRE AND GIRLS INC. CAPSULE COLLECTION (TYPE 2RU)

I learned about this campaign through a conversation with my friend Trisha who works for the jewelry brand, Hearts On Fire. I met Trisha on the bar line at a dog lovers' weekly happy hour in the courtyard of an old jail which was converted into a luxury hotel. Trisha didn't have a dog then, but she does now.

She and her Hearts On Fire colleagues were partnering with Girls Inc., a nonprofit serving young women and inspiring them to be "strong, smart and bold." Hearts On Fire would teach the girls the ins and outs of the jewelry business, while helping them design and market their own Girls Inc. collection.[13] The girls presented their ideas to the Hearts On Fire team, and the jewelry was produced and sold, with a portion of proceeds going to Girls Inc. It led to some outrageous designs the brand had never attempted before, like a ring with diamonds on one side and rubies on the other – the colors of the collaboration partners – which flipped back and forth on a hinge.

Trisha said they wanted to "go beyond just supporting the organization with a financial gift, and go deeper to create an experience that would truly impact these amazing young women. Their creativity reinvigorated my love for the business after more than a decade."

They didn't reinvent jewelry, but they created a special line with a newsworthy story engraved on it from the beginning.

OTHERS

Type 2s are the most common forms of PR Inventions.

- KFC's "Extra Crispy Sunscreen" was a sunscreen which smelled like fried chicken. Was it real? Yes. Was the thing that made it special also useful? No. But it was still fun. Del Taco got there later with "Eau De French Fry," their french fry-scented soap. It marked the launch of the brand's "Fresh Faves" boxes which came with crinkle cut fries.
- JetBlue's "Get Packing!" board game was a custom tabletop game which came with real round-trip plane tickets. It retailed on Amazon for $20 and quickly sold out. Later, other brands like Wendy's got in on the board

game idea with creations like the Dungeons & Dragons-style roleplaying game, "Feast of Legends."
- Burger King's "Dogpper" was a Whopper for dogs. They crossed categories to appeal to a specific audience. The internet's dog culture wolfed it down.
- Michelin teamed up with Vans to create a line of sneakers with the Michelin Man on them. Co-branded merchandise from strange-but-sensible bedfellows doesn't make news on its own. Because a PR brain was behind this, it had a purpose. That purpose was to teach teens about tire safety. The only way you could get these sneakers was by posting a selfie performing the "penny test" to check the depth and safety of your tire tread. With the "Street Tread" campaign, PR took one of the lamest topics to teens and made it cool.[14] Other brands got wise to the sneaker-based PR Invention. The following year, Twix teamed up with shoe influencer The Shoe Surgeon to create "Twix Kicks": a custom Air Jordan whose outer fabric could be ripped open like a candy wrapper, revealing a marbled texture underneath, for the launch of Cookies & Creme Twix. The year after that, Carl's Jr. and Hardee's also worked with The Shoe Surgeon to create "Custom Angus Kicks," complete with a pocket in the tongue tag sized to hold ketchup packets, for the return of the Indulgent Steakhouse Angus Thickburger. Market research experts noted these collaborations were "not intended to drive volume, it's really about getting PR."[15]

IHOP's "Pancizza" was a giant pancake delivered in a pizza box. Useful? No Head-turning. Yes. This breakfast brand launched it to hijack National Pizza Day, and it worked. IHOP repeated this success when it went after burgers. For a while, IHOP was a crew of PR pirates,

---

Illustration 8 "The Hearts on Fire & Girls Inc. Capsule Collection" was created by young women

swooping in to steal other brands' food holidays. It was wonderful to watch.

- Swedish Housing portal Hemnet analyzed what consumers were searching for on their site and built the "House of Clicks" based on what 2 million of them were looking for in a home. PR is enamored with clever uses of data. This was a company taking data it already had and applying it to create something trend-revealing.
- BrewDog created the "Bar on the Edge," a conceptual bar straddling the U.S./Mexico border to unify the two countries during a time of political strife over immigration.
- IKEA's "Soffa Sans" font was a typeface made from the couches in IKEA's online sofa planner, inspired by memes consumers were creating with the planner. The design community loved it.
- State Street Global Advisors and its agency, McCann New York, took a statue of a young woman sculpted by Kristen Visbal for International Women's Day and made it the focal point of a guerilla campaign called "Fearless Girl." The statue stared down the famous Charging Bull of Wall Street, called attention to the finance industry's glass ceiling and promoted State Street's SHE fund of companies with gender diversity in their leadership. It was a blockbuster campaign in the middle of the digital age, and it used a bronze statue. My Syracuse University professor Steve Masiclat once said, "All the means of communication that have been used throughout history remain at our disposal, and each has a best use. For example, we don't regularly carve in stone these days, but when we do, it's for a reason, and the effect is likely to be quite monumental."[16] That was "Fearless Girl." Edward Bernays understood the power of symbolism in PR better than anyone, and it's a cornerstone of some of the best campaigns nearly a century later.

Illustration 9 "Michelin Vans" were created to teach teens about tire pressure

- East West Market's "Embarrassing Plastic Bags" were plastic bags with designs intended to embarrass the carrier for using single-use plastic. It made customers look like they just walked out of an adult video store, a colon care co-op and a wart ointment shop. It backfired a bit when people began collecting them, but at least the collected units didn't go straight into a landfill.

None of these things were new product categories. They didn't *do* anything new. But the novelty baked into them set them up for great stories.

NOTES

1 Spector, Barry and Shelley. *Diverse Voices* (PRSA Foundation, 2020).
2 Cone. "2017 Cone Gen Z CSR Study: How to speak Z" http://conecomm.com/research-blog/2017-genz-csr-study#download-the-research
3 A few times in this book, you'll see the importance of talking it out. It's the process of giving voice to an idea with someone else, and developing it as you talk through it.
4 For all the talk in this book about rule-breaking, crying on cue isn't a bad strategy for getting out of trouble.
5 Something to remember if you're working on an Invention and the person who produced it might be around. Take the time to savor it; you never know if they're watching!
6 Malamut, Melissa. "The Best Healthy Restaurants in Boston" (Bon Appétit, September 11, 2018). http://bonappetit.com/gallery/the-best-healthy-restaurants-in-boston
7 Brar, Faith. "Life Alive's New Back Bay Space is a Fresh New Take on their Local Plant-based Chain (Fitt Boston, May 22, 2019). http://fitt.co/boston/life-alive-brookline/
8 Colby, Celina. "Life Alive Makes Healthy Eating Delicious, Accessible" (Brookline Hub, October 2, 2018). http://brooklinehub.com/life-alive-makes-healthy-eating-delicious-accessible/
9 Babür, Oset. "Panera Founder Has Quietly Launched a Fast-Casual Empire from Boston" (Food & Wine, October 15, 2018). http://foodandwine.com/news/panera-founder-ron-shaich-fast-casual-boston

10 Blumenthal, Rachel Leah. "Life Alive Will Bring Its Vegetable-Packed Grain Bowls to Back Bay Next" (Eater Boston, September 19, 2018). http://boston.eater.com/2018/9/19/17879512/life-alive-back-bay-expansion-boylston-street

11 Louise, J.Q. "Tasty Thanksgiving Dishes, Tips from the Pros" (The Boston Herald, November 19, 2018). http://bostonherald.com/2018/11/14/tasty-thanksgiving-dishes-tips-from-the-pros/

12 Adam Ritchie Brand Direction. "Mix It Up – Campaign Sizzle Reel (Official)" (YouTube). http://youtu.be/z5_hKywhtbU

13 Hearts On Fire. "Hearts On Fire and Girls Inc." (YouTube). http://youtu.be/VakdRvvOEEk

14 Incredibly, the PR agency behind this idea lost the Michelin account soon after. Even the best ideas, well-executed, can't prevent an agency change. But a year later, Michelin came back to that agency and asked if they'd be interested in working together again.

15 NPD Group Senior Industry Advisor of Sports Matt Powell in an interview with Jessica Wohl. "How Carl's Jr. and Hardee's are Jumping on the Branded Sneaker Trend" (Ad Age, April 19, 2021). http://adage.com/article/cmo-strategy/carls-jr-and-hardees-aim-whetsneaker-fans-appetites-unique-kicks/2329246

16 Spoken to his GRA 217 class in Spring 2001.

TYPE III
TRANSFORMATION

"No idea is too stupid."

– *Amanda Byrne, PR pro*[1]

An Invention in PR Type 3 is transformation: turning something everyday into something extraordinary.

This is the story of "The M.O.M. Squad."

THE M.O.M. SQUAD (TYPE 3CU)

By now, you've seen why your first trigger pull should always be aimed at the audacious.

This project began when our new baby gear client's biggest retailer, Babies"R"Us, had just gone out of business. The atmosphere around Summer Infant was uneasy.

DOI: 10.4324/9781003216872-5

They had a new baby monitor, and asked how we'd support it. The product was already baked. Done. We connected too late in the game to invent one. But it was our first big project for them, and it had to be good. We needed another approach.

This new monitor had a feature which would alert the caregiver if the baby or something else crossed an invisible safety boundary surrounding the crib. We could have fun with that.

Their new brand promise was about taking the parenting experience "from merely manageable to a bit magical."

It was December, so the first place we went was, "How can parents use this monitor to catch Santa? Could it be pointed at the chimney, under the tree or at the plate of milk and cookies?" Next was, "Santa is just one of many magical creatures which require monitoring. Which other magical creatures could we expand this to? Bigfoot? Chupacabra? The Jersey Devil? Aliens? The Loch Ness Monster?" Then it became, "What if we seeded the monitor to the animal control centers closest to where they're frequently sighted?" We'd equip the centers for the search and care of these special creatures. The campaign images would display Mama Sasquatch and baby Sasquatches traipsing across a wooded path like "Make Way for Ducklings" on a monitor screen. And when the search was over, the units could be donated to a local family. The only catch would be the family would have to believe!

The client took a pass. They didn't want to see anything potentially scary on a monitor screen, even if it was a friendly sort of cartoon-scary.

Maybe I'd seen too many episodes of "The X-Files." Marketing expert John Hegarty said, "You cannot create great work unless a little bit of you goes into it."[2] Sometimes too much of you goes into it and you're pulled by the fun of it. How much fun would it have been to send baby monitors to unsuspecting animal control centers from Scotland to Japan, and tell that story? To introduce a touch of cuddly Cryptozoology to the baby gear world?

Ideas are more like first dates than relationships. Unless you know in your bones that it's going to work, don't go down in flames over it. And don't let it be watered down by committee. Let it go, allow the client to give you a second prompt and see if it leads to something better.

Jen, Summer Infant's VP, Brand Marketing, said parents wanted to be superheroes to their children. Their tagline was, "Baby has you. You have us."

Superheroes. That was the trigger.

At the time, movie marquees were filled with superhero films. Families of all backgrounds were lining up to see them. We did a little poking around and learned women and men were equally excited about superhero movies. "Wonder Woman" just became the top-grossing superhero origin movie of all time and "Black Panther" had crossed the $1 billion mark. Audiences were asking for greater diversity and more women in these films.

This time we came up with a concept that would tap into that superhero trend, the empowering message of the women's movement and break through with an unforgettable visual. We were going to create a pregnant superhero. A woman with top-notch gadgetry to heighten her powers. She'd be Batman with a baby bump, and nothing would stand in her way.

What's crazier? A baby Loch Ness Monster or a pregnant superhero? Maybe it came down to what's more on-trend and a better brand fit.

A member of the client team asked if the concept risked offending women who couldn't get pregnant. It was worth considering, but a baby brand who can't talk about pregnancy runs a greater risk of painting itself into a corner.

We reached out to Marvel Entertainment about a collaboration with one of their artists. They offered the brand a paid partnership it couldn't afford. But it didn't mean the end of the idea. Getting Marvel onboard was always going to be a stretch. You should always aim for the stars, even when it's a shot in the dark. We were just getting started. We'd create the superhero ourselves if we needed to.

Just one superhero? Maybe not. The client enjoyed the idea so much, they wanted multiple characters. If we did that, the group would need a memorable name. Band them together and brand them together. What would you call the world's first team of pregnant superheroes, who'd come from all walks of life and all stages of pregnancy to kick butt and celebrate all moms as heroes to their little ones ("Baby has you"), who would each be equipped with a Summer Infant product as her tool of choice: a monitor, a potty, a stroller and a bath seat? ("You have us"), who'd be the living embodiment of the brand message?

Jen's team suggested calling the group, "The M.O.M. Squad." It already sounded like a hit. To name the individual characters, we asked our friends, beginning with the character equipped with the baby monitor. Should she be called "The Motherboard?" My friend Matt suggested "Momitor," and "Agent Momitor" came online. We wanted a super strong one who could push anything with her Summer Infant stroller. My friend Rishava texted, "Motherlode" and "The MotherLoad" was born. The client came up with "Aquamom" who had a bath seat and "Professor Potty" who had a training toilet.

That's the value in talking through your ideas with your people. Let others react and see what it brings.

We wanted the characters to break old comic book stereotypes of women being drawn by men, so we asked Summer Infant to hire a female comic book artist. Their video partner suggested Viera Boudreau. Her style and attitude were perfect to bring "The M.O.M. Squad" to life with powerful art that would turn heads.

Not long before Viera put her pen to tablet, something hit us which could take it to the next level: what if we based each character on a real-life pregnant woman with her own story to tell? And not just any pregnant women: pregnant micro-influencers. And not just from one market: they'd come from across the country. And not just geographically strategic pregnant micro-influencers: they'd also be culturally diverse. Doing this would bring a concept based in fantasy into reality.

A member of the client team expressed concern about the campaign continuing to evolve that far into the game. Jen saw the 'real people' tweak for what it was and helped the rest of the client team understand why it was an upgrade. This is how good concepts get made. They don't always arrive fully formed on the page. We can't all be Frank Lloyd Wright drafting Fallingwater in one sitting. You can sell an idea, but once you get deep into the work, you can't help but notice ways to make it stronger. Concepts are upgraded as far as time and budget allow. The motor is tuned right up until the car leaves the racing pit, and even after it's left. It helps to have an ally managing the pit crew who knows how races are won and goes to bat for you.

This move is also what made the campaign become the third slice of Invention in PR. It was a Type 3: transformation. Invention by way of transforming the everyday into the extraordinary, in one move. With the opportunity to invent a product off the table, we invented something else. In this case, it was transforming pregnant women into the world's first team of pregnant comic book superheroes.

We outlined the criteria for the four women who would make up the group and shared it with Summer Infant. Paige, the brand's Digital Engagement Manager, wasted no time finding incredible women who fit the bill and bringing them onboard.

One last hurdle: the biggest trade show in the industry was right around the corner. All hands were on deck for the conference, and "The M.O.M. Squad" had to wait. Between press briefings at the show, I sat with Jen and Paige in their booth, and storyboarded the launch trailer with them. Then it was back to more press briefings, knowing what we were cooking up was every bit as exciting as the new products we were showing.

When we got back from the event, the clock was ticking. It had to be content creation at the speed of pop culture. A one-day shoot yielded the video trailer[3] introducing the campaign and showing Viera morphing the real women into their pregnant superhero alter egos. The call-to-action invited consumers to share and tag the supermoms in their own lives. To connect with moms and moms-to-be, the campaign would shine a light on the superhero in each of them.

Summer Infant launched a microsite where consumers were asked to tag their personal supermoms. Three consumers would receive the full line of products used by the heroes and Summer Infant gift cards.

Most campaigns are brand- or product-focused. This campaign was designed to be both. Most campaigns focus on a single holiday. This campaign used a pair of holidays as goalposts to land results between. It would kick off just before National Superhero Day (April 28) and culminate on Mother's Day (May 13). The superhero holiday happening

n that window was pure serendipity, and we made the most
)f it. We had two timely news hooks, which always helps,
)ecause reporters tend to ignore something the first time it's
)ut in front of them.

Ne went back to Marvel a second time and asked if they'd
)e willing to amplify Summer Infant's positive announcement
)n their social platforms for Mother's Day. They declined
gain, so we went back and wrote a different take on a news
elease,[4] making it an open letter to Marvel, extolling the
irtues of pregnant superheroes and inviting them to write
uture M.O.M. Squad adventures together with Summer
nfant. It was a lighthearted note to boost media interest and
he brand's search engine optimization.

Nith all the pieces in place, we had only two-and-a-half
veeks to conduct the outreach.

Moments after the trailer was finalized, we offered it as an
xclusive to the most influential online parenting outlet in
he country: The Bump. Once they broke the news,[5] we
ised that Bump placement as proof-of-concept to propel the
tory out of parenting media, and into outlets in lifestyle,
vomen's, pop culture, news and business media, with angles
or each.

A funny thing about that Bump story. We felt like it was
 home run right out of the gate. It premiered the concept
ationally, profiled each superhero in detail and included
mages and backlinks for readers to purchase each of
heir corresponding products. When we proudly sent it
ver, a member of the client's social media team asked,
 Does the Bump share this information anywhere else?" It
vas a reminder that even when you've just served up the
est possible sales-driving coverage on the most credible

---

lustration 10   "The M.O.M. Squad," Summer Infant's team of
regnant comic book superheroes

and trafficked news site for the target audience, to some
marketers, it doesn't count unless it's also hitting social. (It
soon did.)

As the outreach continued, we offered the inspirational
women behind "The M.O.M. Squad" characters for
interviews, along with Viera and Jen, and suggested editors
might engage readers by asking what their own superpowers
might be. This helped us sell the pitch.

We secured stories across six different media segments and
reached 93.3 million target consumers. The messaging
included Summer Infant's message of support. "Summer
Infant supports you" (The Bump). "Summer Infant's mission
to sing moms' praises is an overdue and important one"
(What To Expect).[6] "This innovative brand is all about
family" (Celebrity Baby Trends).[7] "Summer Infant has
taken the superhero concept to the next level" (New York
Family).[8] "What I love about this campaign are the stories
being told and the conversations being started" (GeekMom).[9]
"Illustrative and empowering" (Trend Hunter).[10] "Who can't
get behind a little mom-as-superhero action this Mother's
Day?" (The Washington Post).[11] Viera's show-stopping
artwork ran front and center in every story.

Occasionally an editor surprises you and sums up the
effort better than you could. My favorite quote was from
GirlTalkHQ, who said, "This badass team of comic book
characters gives heroism a whole new perspective....it [could]
challenge the way our society thinks about mothers."[12]
I immediately wished we could turn back the clock and use
a version of this from the beginning without sounding full of
ourselves. Reshaping perceptions of pregnant women? Holy
moly. Thank you.

"The M.O.M. Squad" doubled the brand's social media
interactions from the previous period and reached 5.4 million
target consumers. It struck a chord with people who tagged

their own supermoms and said, "Hannelore Moore literally is a super hero already! Love you Hanni! xoxo." "Stephanie Stevens you are a superhero Mom to those charming boys!!" "Alex Umstead! We are totes M.O.M. squad superheroes!!!" M.O.M. Squad members posted their characters and said, "I am in tears seeing this actually come to life!"

Summer Infant ran the email, Facebook and YouTube TrueView campaign. In a week, the combined earned and paid efforts drove 29,934 YouTube views (70 times the brand's previous video performance), a 56.40% view rate (retail benchmark: 15.7%), a 10% email open rate and a 6% clickthrough rate. The story spread and generated 3,974 landing page sessions. Coverage backlinked to each product's purchase page. Sales increased 13.3% that quarter.

Months after the campaign, its assets were still being shared by consumers around the world. When that happens, it's proof you've tapped into something universal.

Even though it didn't get to create the products this time, PR was the discipline which sparked the creative process, marshaled the client's internal resources and drove an inter-agency team to carry a transformative idea across disciplines and channels. The client called it "inspiring...an excellent return on investment...generated excitement within the organization" and added, "The brand had not received this level of coverage [in all of its 33 years]."[13]

Again, there were no big names or big spends. Just a celebration of the heroics of everyday women, elevating them to superhero status and helping a brand recover its superpowers.[14]

After the sun set on our heroes, "The M.O.M. Squad" also did well in industry competitions. The following year, an agency owned by one of the largest holding companies in the world appeared to replicate its strategy, right down to the mix of heroes, the language and even a female comic book artist. They also entered it in the same industry competitions where "The M.O.M. Squad" was honored the previous year. Some people talk about having to top themselves with each project. We were forced to beat an apparent copy of our work – sometimes in the same competition categories – with our next piece of work.

It felt a little strange. When we confronted the agency about it, they were unapologetic. Instead of changing our agency's tagline to "Ideas worth stealing," we saw the humor in one of the world's biggest players appearing to take its cues from one of the world's smallest. It reaffirmed what we were doing. If our ideas were good enough to be copied, why wouldn't brands and even other agencies hire us to teach them how to come up with them on their own?' So, we developed an idea creation training service called "Mission Control,"[15] and turned lemons into lemonade.

If we could go back, we would have loved to bring live events into the picture, like M.O.M. Squad characters appearing at comic conventions, and an app where you could turn yourself into a pregnant comic book superhero. Maybe we would have made M.O.M. Squad action figures and a physical comic book. Or done a version for dads and ultimately brought them both together to form a super-supergroup. Maybe someday we'll get to.

At the time, we were already focused on the next concept. The company needed a news hook for a consumer event in New York City. We said, "Make it super high-end, but only invite people if they have fewer than 5,000 social followers and call it an 'Influencer Inversion.'"[16]

Then they had a six-month-old high-definition monitor that needed help, so we said, "Let's hire the guy who went viral Photoshopping his daughter into precarious situations, show

the heart-stopping moments which were happening in the
nursery all along, but were always hidden from us pre-high-def,
and call it 'Caught in the Act: The Secret Lives of Babies.'"[17]

The success of "The M.O.M. Squad" earned us the client's
trust. And we still got to put something crazy on a baby
monitor screen after all!

THE TAMPON BOOK (TYPE 3RU)

This Invention in PR, Type 3, was done by the German
agency Scholz & Friends for its online retailer client, The
Female Company. They knew it was nonsense that tampons
were subject to a luxury tax, so they packaged the tampons
in a book, filled it with literature educating consumers on the
unfairness of the tax, called it "The Tampon Book," earned
international media around it, and sold every copy they
produced.

It ultimately helped change policy. Tampons in Germany are
no longer subject to a luxury tax.

It also won the Cannes Lions PR Lions Grand Prix. It's both
an Invention in PR Type 1 and Type 3. It turned something
into something else, had a unique function which served a
purpose, solved a problem, raised awareness and changed
behavior.

Three years later, Tim Hortons appeared to take a page
from this incredible campaign with its thoughtfully designed
"Mother's Day Donut Disguise Box": a box of donuts
repackaged to look like books, with titles like "Glazed
Expectations" and "Twenty Thousand Timbits Under the
Sea." It was cute, but it was no "Tampon Book." Good
Inventions in PR are frequently imitated, but the copies never
seem to have the same punch.

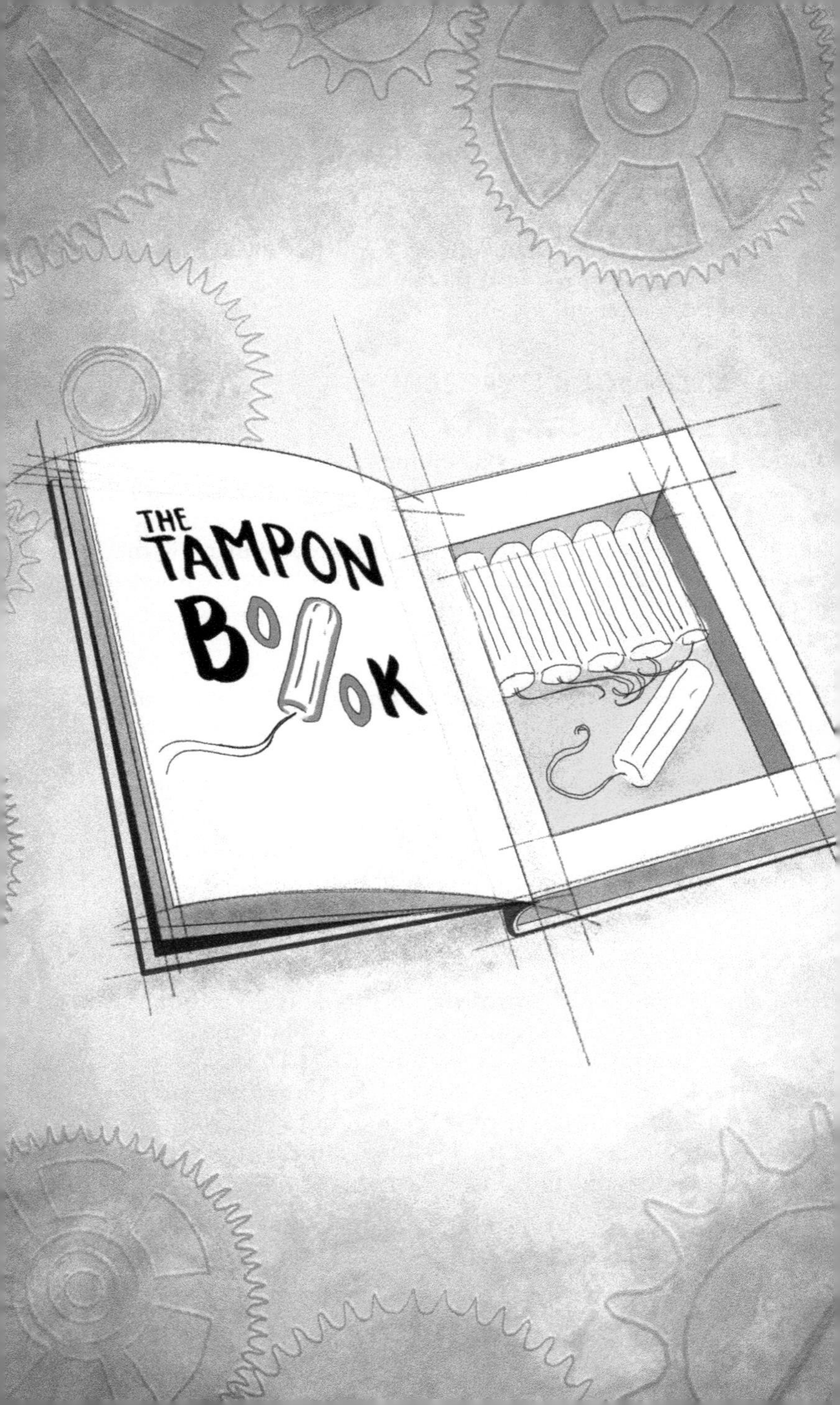
THE TAMPON BOOK

OTHERS

The easy way to remember transformation is to think in terms of turning nouns into other nouns. "The M.O.M. Squad" transformed a *person* (pregnant women). "The Walking Dead" example we're about to share transformed a *place* (a New York City sidewalk). "The Tampon Book" transformed a *thing* (a tampon). Extreme makeovers fascinate people, and a well-planned Type 3 can reach beyond the makeover to make something new.

AMC transformed a New York City sidewalk into a zombie bit to promote the season premiere of "The Walking Dead." A sidewalk wasn't the product, but it was an everyday thing where they could literally embed their greatest brand asset – zombies – and add a layer of surrealism to a walk down the street.

7-Eleven stores were transformed into Kwik-E-Marts to promote "The Simpsons Movie." The *movie* came out a long time ago, but the *move* is timeless.

Degage Ministries is a religion-based organization focusing on homelessness. It did a before-and-after with a homeless veteran, turning him into a clean-cut, distinguished-looking job candidate. They showed everyone not to judge a book by its cover.

Crispin Porter + Bogusky made the hilarious "Professionals Collection" for Fruit of the Loom, where they transformed athletic wear into eye-popping formal wear. You had to look twice to see that these were actually sweats.

Budweiser turned spent plastic cups from a Russian soccer tournament into a soccer field in Sochi. It was the perfect visual accompaniment to their sustainability pledge to brew beer using renewable electricity.

Hill Holliday transformed the idea of a bakery into a pop-up shop selling cupcakes with matches, nails and

Illustration 11　"The Tampon Book" from The Female Company helped change an unfair tax policy

scorpions for the nonprofits Celiac Disease Foundation
and Beyond Celiac. The faux store was created to help
people understand what having Celiac Disease feels like
for sufferers.

- Arby's transformed ground turkey into a carrot and called
it a "Marrot." This "megetable" was also a new category
of product.
- Metallica was transformed into an illustrated children's
book called "The ABCs of Metallica" for their workforce
education cause and to promote their tour.
- Cheez-It crackers and House Wine made a combination
box to reinforce the message that the crackers are made
with real cheese. They faced a similar challenge, where the
product already existed. They couldn't change it, so they
changed something else and made a creative combination.
- Street Grace is a nonprofit that works to stop the
commercial exploitation of children. Its "Stop Traffick"
campaign transformed 72 school busses – enough to fit
the 3,600 Georgia children sold every year – into a mile-
long moving billboard displaying sex trafficking statistics.
The route ended at the football stadium where the Super
Bowl was about to be held. It led to 33 sex trafficking
arrets in the month after the event.
- Remember Edward Bernays? He didn't reinvent Ivory
soap, but in 1923 he got schoolchildren to transform
Ivory soap into something interesting by artfully carving
millions of bars. Ivory soap was Ivory soap. It already
existed. Bernays transformed those ordinary bars of soap
into sculpture.

For each of these examples, something everyday was turned
into something that would turn heads.

Illustration 12   AMC promoted "The Walking Dead" by transforming
a city sidewalk into a zombie pit

NOTES

1 Amanda Byrne from Ogilvy in a conversation with Adam Ritchie at Mariel, November 20, 2019.

2 Hegarty, John. *Hegarty on Advertising* (Thames Hudson 2011).

3 Summer Infant. "The World's First Team of Pregnant Superheroes" (YouTube). http://youtu.be/9JVhpiHiOoU

4 Summer Infant. "The World's First Team of Pregnant Superheroes is Born" (PRWeb, April 26, 2018). http://prweb.com/releases/2018/04/prweb15443216.htm

5 Arsenault, Anisa. "4 Real-Life Moms Get a Superhero Alter Ego" (The Bump, April 26, 2018). http://thebump.com/news/summer-infant-superhero-moms

6 Brown, Maressa. "There's a New Squad of Pregnant Superheroes in Town and It's About Time" (What To Expect, May 9, 2018). http://whattoexpect.com/news/pregnancy/pregnant-superheroes-summer-infant/

7 Mellinger, Gloria. "Saturday is National Superhero Day – the Perfect Time to Celebrate Your Supermom!" (Celebrity Baby Trends, April 27, 2018). http://celebritybabytrends.com/this-saturday-is-national-superhero-day-celebrate-your-supermom

8 Guidry, Kelly. "Meet the First Team of Pregnant Superheroes, Inspired by Real Life Moms (New York Family, May 11, 2018). http://newyorkfamily.com/meet-the-first-team-of-pregnant-superheroes-inspired-by-real-life-moms/

9 Moulton, Kali. "Moms Are Super: Meet the M.O.M. Squad" (GeekMom, May 13, 2018). http://geekmom.com/2018/05/moms-are-super-meet-the-m-o-m-squad/

10 Smith, Ellen. "Mom-Inspired Superhero Leagues" (Trend Hunter, May 22, 2018). http://trendhunter.com/trends/mom-squad

11 Joyce, Amy. "These moms were given their own superhero personas. What's your superpower?" (The Washington Post, May 13, 2018). http://washingtonpost.com/news/parenting/wp/2018/05/13/these-moms-were-given-their-own-superhero-personas-whats-your-superpower/

12 Dahya, Asha. "World's First Team of Pregnant Superheroes Celebrating Motherhood This Mother's Day" (GirlTalkHQ, May 10, 2018). http://girltalkhq.com/worlds-first-team-of-pregnant-superheroes-celebrating-motherhood-this-mothers-day/

13 Summer Infant VP, Brand Marketing Jen Johnson in an email to Adam Ritchie, May 14, 2018.

14 Adam Ritchie Brand Direction. "The M.O.M. Squad – Campaign Sizzle Reel (Official)" (YouTube). http://youtu.be/sqF1nLsCvxc

15 Adam Ritchie Brand Direction. "Mission Control" http://aritchbrand.com/missioncontrol

16 born free. "Why Should Influencers Have All the Fun?" (PRWeb, May 22, 2019). http://prweb.com/releases/why_should_influencers_have_all_the_fun/prweb16328293.htm

17 Piñon, Natasha. "World's greatest (Photoshop) dad strikes again" (Mashable, October 21, 2019). http://mashable.com/article/photoshop-dad-returns

MISSES

"I get paid to try."

– *Adam Lewis, PR pro*[1]

Success isn't guaranteed with an Invention-first approach. Sometimes it backfires. As brands elbow their way into conversations where they weren't necessarily invited, a number of them also manage to bring the wrong thing to the party.

Burger King partnered with Mental Health America to create "Real Meals" because "No one is happy all the time." It featured the Pissed Meal, Blue Meal, Salty Meal, YAAAS Meal and DGAF Meal. CNBC[2] challenged Burger King's place in the mental health discussion. I wondered about the wisdom of using a nonprofit as a shield while attacking a competitor.

DOI: 10.4324/9781003216872-6

Mattel released its "Barbie Dia De Muertos Doll" to celebrate the Day of the Dead, a Mexican holiday honoring departed loved ones. CNN[3] questioned if it crossed the line into cultural appropriation. At a time when immigration raids and families being separated at the border were in the news, there was an unignorable risk of appearing to commercialize a solemn 3,000-year-old Mexican tradition with a $75 light-skinned American doll.[4]

When Brita, the water filter brand, released a line of ugly holiday sweaters, it appeared to go against its own message. The sweaters were made from recycled plastic, and Fast Company[5] pointed out why corny holiday sweaters were bad for the environment, since they're often purchased, worn once for laughs, then discarded.

"The Glenlivet Capsule Collection," whiskey in clear edible pods, was made with eco-friendly materials and launched for London Cocktail Week. The brand was trying to create a new category of on-the-go "glassless cocktails" but wound up devaluing the product, building a mental association with laundry detergent pods, as reported in The New York Times[6] and creating a short-run item which risked long-term brand damage.

Sometimes an apparent success is really a brand recycling an old idea and failing to evolve it. When Pizza Hut reintroduced its "Triple Threat Box," a triple-decker cardboard delivery box with three pizza drawers, five years after its debut, it earned positive coverage. But they could have kicked it up a notch by at least adding another drawer for consumers who needed an extra pie in an extra tough year. When their competitor, Domino's, was eating their creative lunch with outstanding service-based Inventions like "Domino's Baby Registry" and "Paving For Pizza," it would have been nice to see Pizza Hut pulling something fresh out of the oven instead of serving up cold leftovers.

If a brand has deep pockets, it can invent an intentional miss with the aim of getting sued. Lil Nas X rolled out "Satan Shoes" using the Nike Air Max 97 platform and a drop of human blood to promote a video where he gives a lap dance to the devil. Nike predictably sued him and extended the story's shelf life with follow-up coverage beyond the announcement.

Speaking of human blood in an Invention in PR Type 2, the rock band, KISS, mixed their own blood into the red ink for their "KISS Marvel Comic Book" in 1977. This same move was still shocking nearly half a century later when Lil Nas X did it with unidentified blood. Before giving too much credit to a new idea, the odds are high that a version of it came before, and it was probably done by Gene Simmons.

Established brands can be a little lazy on the Invention front. When you're working with something already famous, just about any Invention you roll out will earn a degree of attention. They're coming up short on true creativity, problem-solving and the opportunity to do something meaningful. The most daring Inventions in PR are when a brand nobody's heard of concocts something which puts them on the map for the first time in their history, or when a true challenger brand plays way outside of its turf. Heinz combining two existing flavors – mayo and ketchup to make "Mayochup," or ketchup and ranch to make "Kranch" – is weak sauce by comparison.[7]

For a big crossover collaboration product, you need big clout. Big brands tend to pair off with other big brands. But if you're working on a smaller brand, you can still pull off a great crossover by hooking up with another brand at the same level. When you find a partner your size, you can still

---

Illustration 13 Mattel's "Barbie Dia De Muertos Doll" drew accusations of appropriation

reap the same major earned media benefits as long as you land on something interesting, and really work the story.

You could fill a warehouse with products that failed. Someone even did. A research firm in Ann Arbor, Michigan called NewProductWorks created a private, clients-only collection of new product failures, like Gerber's attempt at creating baby food for adults in its iconic jars.

We've had our own fails which never left the drafting table. Sell-in isn't guaranteed. You might run a concept past multiple brands before finding a partner that acknowledges its potential. Carol Cone, who we met earlier, said of any big idea, "You get nine nos before you get a yes."[8]

Even after the deal is done, your Invention can still be nixed.

We once had marketing VPs from two well-known brands geared up to build something unique together, and just before the parts were ordered, one of the brands got cold feet. Making matters worse, it was our own client who backed out, not the brand we'd worked hard to bring onboard. Heads of marketing aren't always enough. To guarantee the project, you need buy-in from the very top.

A lot of it comes down to the personality and interests of the person up there. They need to feel like they can wrap themselves in the idea. Bring them a concept they'd love telling a party guest who asks, "Hey Jane, what are you and Brand X up to these days?" and you're halfway there.

Sometimes I'm asked to define Invention-based success. What does it look like? Is it sales? Is it a knowledge, opinion or behavior change among the target audience? It can be all those things. But with Invention, internal stakeholders need to see success as the Invention simply existing.

Remember Ben, the brewery co-founder from the beer can album campaign? He would have been happy if it never earned a speck of media. He just wanted to do it. Some Inventions are just worth doing. Even if it falls short of its business objectives, everyone involved should be able to look back and say, "We're glad we made that." If every campaign was held to the fire over its likelihood of hitting key performance indicators before it got the green light, the world would be missing a lot of powerful work.

Inventions are experiments, and come with the risks and rewards of experimentation. You can go in armed with the right insights indicating a strong likelihood of success, but there are no guarantees. You can't be daring and bank on a sure thing at the same time. If you want to work this path, eventually you'll need to climb your own version of the cherry picker basket from the Prologue, check your safety harness and jump.

All the ideas in this book, even the misses, were successful on some level. Someone saw an opportunity to do something unusual and got enough people to say "yes." That's a win, even when it fails.

In this chapter, we saw Inventions causing a degree of crisis. In the next chapter, we'll look at brands inventing their way out of one.

NOTES

1 Adam Lewis from The Planetary Group in a conversation with Adam Ritchie at Anchovies (March 30, 2018).
2 Graham, Megan. "Burger King faces backlash after linking ad campaign to mental health, showing the risks of cause-based marketing" (CNBC, May 3, 2019). http://cnbc.com/2019/05/03/burger-king-faces-backlash-after-linking-ad-campaign-to-mental-health.html
3 Heyward, Giulia and Ries, Brian. "Some say a 'Day of the Dead' Barbie is guilty of cultural appropriation. Its designer says it is celebrating tradition" (CNN, November 1, 2020). http://cnn.com/2020/11/01/us/day-of-the-dead-barbie-cultural-appropriation-trnd/index.html

4 If this was a Type 2 miss, the brand's life-size "Barbie Malibu Dreamhouse" in partnership with Airbnb was a Type 3 hit – even if it came to life a few months after the more ambitious Type 3, "The Bell," a Taco Bell hotel, opened its doors in Palm Springs.

5 Segran, Elizabeth. "For the love of God, don't buy that ugly Christmas sweater" (Fast Company, December 17, 2019). http://fastcompany.com/90443839/
for-the-love-of-god-dont-buy-that-ugly-christmas-sweater

6 Fortin, Jacey. "Edible Whisky Pods Cause 'a Bit of a Stir' With Scotch Fans" (New York Times, October 7, 2019). http://nytimes.com/2019/
10/07/business/glenlivet-whisky-scotch-pods.html

7 Most Inventions in PR are food and beverage-related. The made-to-order nature of that industry makes them the easiest to pull off. The effort that goes into making a food item isn't as intense as what goes into getting a packaged good on the shelf. I've tried to keep the F&B examples to a minimum because they're so frequent – particularly in fast food.

8 Cone, Carol. "Innovator 25" (PRovoke, October 2019). http://provokemedia.com/ranking-and-data/innovator-25/
innovator-25-2019/innovator-25-americas-2019/carol-cone

INVENTION IN A CRISIS

" We are continually faced with great opportunities which are brilliantly disguised as unsolvable problems."
– Margaret Mead, Anthropologist

ʼR teams known for their creativity and PR teams known
or their crisis management abilities don't always run in the
ame circles. Clients don't hire heart surgeons when they're in
he market for brain surgeons. For Invention-led campaigns,
here's a lot one can learn from the other.

ᴀ materials shortage can be a major crisis. When KFC
ᴀn low on chicken in the UK, it could have laid out the
ᴀcts leading to the shortage, expressed its commitment
ɔ consumers, reassured them with platitudes and bored
ᴴem to death. Instead, KFC took it as an opportunity
ɔ conceptually transform their packaging so their iconic
ᴴicken bucket read, "FCK" instead of "KFC." They ran it
ᴺ a full-page ad and emerged from the ordeal with more

DOI: 10.4324/9781003216872-7

IT IS TWO MINUTES
TO MIDNIGHT

brand love than before. Bud Light also showed an ability to go beyond predictable conflict communication when Modist Brewing Company appeared to infringe on its intellectual property by selling a brew called "Dilly Dilly IPA." Rather than the soulless cease-and-desist letter most consumers would expect from a large corporation, it transformed the letter into a parchment proclamation read by an actor playing a town crier in Modist's Minneapolis taproom, earning itself a viral hit worthy of PR legend Arthur Page's principle to always remain good-humored.[1]

Some brands use invention and transformation to address crises bigger than themselves. Honey Nut Cheerios made shoppers pause in the cereal aisle when it transformed its packaging to remove its Buzz Bee mascot to raise awareness of declining bee populations. The Urgent Love substance abuse initiative invented "Opi's," a conceptual line of gear for babies struggling from withdrawal during the opioid crisis. As the world entered the nuclear age and humanity itself appeared to be in crisis, the Bulletin of the Atomic Scientists came up with "The Doomsday Clock" to track the likelihood of a man-made global catastrophe. To this day, every time it ticks, the world watches. These examples are all symbolic and show the power of the imaginary in crises which are alarmingly real.

Someday a reader might pick up this book with COVID-19 as distant a cultural memory as the Spanish Flu was to my generation. A lot of the people who lived through it would prefer to forget about it. But history teaches us there will always be another pandemic, so let's explore how brands used invention and transformation to work their way through that particular global crisis, even when resources were tight.

Illustration 14   "The Doomsday Clock" from the Bulletin of the Atomic Scientists counts the symbolic minutes until a man-made global catastrophe

Early in the pandemic, when hand sanitizer was scarce, the Chinese Canadian National Council for Social Justice created its own line of sanitizer to stop the spread of xenophobic behavior toward the Asian community. Distilleries were transforming their spirits production into sanitizer production, the same way breweries transform beer production into canned water production during natural disasters. They asked themselves, "What's the hot commodity right now? What point could we make with our own version of it? If we make it, will it rub off on our brand in a positive way?"

Speaking of hot commodities, toilet paper was a big one. Shoppers were fighting over it. You don't see a lot of Invention from the B2B world. But that didn't stop NCSolutions, a company that uses consumer shopping data to help other companies improve their advertising efficiency. They launched the "National TP Index": an ongoing tool to track where toilet paper stood in daily consumer dollars spent. Toilet paper usually hangs out in 20th to 30th place, but it skyrocketed to first place in COVID-19 month one. They announced it on their website with the headline: "Butt Seriously: The TP Index," showing a sense of humor also rare in B2B programming.[2]

During the initial lockdown, the dating app Bumble partnered with Babe Wine to help couples break up and move on – literally – with a new service which gave you wine, paid for your moving expenses, helped build your dating profile and deleted all traces of your ex from your phone. A lesser PR brain would have only sent free wine to broken-up quarantiners and called it a campaign to drown sorrows. This team created an entirely new service to promote its existing products and services. They became crisis inventors.

When football fans were desperately missing the experience of pregaming in a parking lot, Pepsi transformed a New York Jets fanatic's yard into a scaled-down replica of the stadium tailgate experience, complete with a paved lot, a light tower and a painted end zone. The photos released with the campaign showed aerial views of a cookie-cutter suburban yard magically turning into a stadium lot. Even though it only happened on one small parcel of land in an otherwise unremarkable town, the story was picked up by news outlets across the country.

When COVID-19 cancelled the Summer Olympics, Arby's created the "Greek Gyro Games": an immersive 8-bit video game where consumers played an unathletic Arby's employee running to relight a gyro spit. Players received free food for completing it, but first they had to earn it by engaging with a brand's crisis creation at great length.

As travel became impossible, an indie bookstore in Dallas called The Wild Detectives transformed itself into a travel agency. Hang on. Why would one of the hardest-to-sustain businesses turn itself into a then-impossible-to-sustain business? It was a conceptual Invention in PR: a microsite offering to transport you to exciting destinations for the absurdly low price of a book. The destinations were the settings of famous books, and the transportation took place in your mind. We call this move the "pivot" or the "zag." It was a smart, positive campaign that zagged in just the right way at the right time.

When face coverings became part of everyday life, most brands slapped their logo on a mask and called it a day. Brands serious about crisis invention took it to the next level. Burger King's "Safe Order Mask" let consumers place their favorite drive-thru order on the front of their mask. And Hormel's "Bacon Mask" smelled like bacon instead of the wearer's bad breath.

If you weren't grabbing something to go, you were cooking or baking at home. So, T-Mobile teamed up with Betty Crocker to create a three-layer "Supercharged 5G Un-carrier Layer Cake Mix" to explain the three spectrum bands of 5G.

In non-pandemic times, every beer brand has a swag cooler. COVID-19 created an opportunity to make them remarkable. During the second pandemic winter, Swedish beer brand Norrlands Ljus studied the output of the summer solstice sun and placed a therapy lamp replicating it inside of a branded cooler, to help Swedes cope with seasonal darkness and social isolation. Not to be outdone, Dos Equis made the "Seis-Foot Cooler": a six-foot-long beer cooler so beer lovers could enjoy a cold one six feet apart.

As stay-at-home orders wore on, puzzles soared in popularity. Heinz made a challenging 570-piece "Ketchup Puzzle" all in red. They didn't reinvent the puzzle, but they created a crisis-ready version with news in the recipe.

Eventually, pajamas became everyone's default loungewear. People who were housebound took to wearing them all day. Understanding this, 7-Eleven Sweden came out with a line of pajamas in its signature colors to mark the launch of its all-day breakfast.

When workers grew tired of their kitchen tables, Nissan stacked the COVID-19 trends of remote work and people spending more time outdoors with its "Caravan Office Pod," a Type 1 concept car with a retractable workspace.

As restrictions eased and life slowly resumed, people were eager to shed their lockdown locks. Heineken rolled out "Heineken Haircuts": mobile hair studios parked outside pubs where a celebrity stylist would give patrons a clip while they sipped a beer.

You didn't need to be a wealthy or famous brand to pull off a good COVID-19 crisis invention. Plenty of smaller brands did it with timely, visually compelling ideas and the commitment to see them through.

A small restaurant in Ocean City, MD called Fish Tales Bar & Grill made national headlines with its "Bumper Tables": giant inner tubes with an eating surface, worn around the waist and mounted on wheels so patrons could socialize while adhering to physical distancing guidelines. A bakery in Rochester, NY called Donuts Delite sold out of donuts featuring edible portraits of beloved health figure and National Institute of Allergy and Infectious Diseases Director Dr. Anthony Fauci. In both cases the visual sold the invention, whether it was innertube-adorned diners or a famous face framed in icing.

Audio was the medium of choice for a bar in Monterrey, Mexico called Maverick. They created a microsite with movable faders allowing visitors to mix the sounds of a bartender working, people talking, rain hitting a window, street ambiance and more "to keep you company while this awful pandemic, which profoundly affects our industry throughout the world, finally passes and we can meet again safely."[3]

You're allowed to have fun with crisis inventions. In some situations, you're even allowed to be cute.

We had our own pandemic concepts, which we labeled COVIDEA. We wanted Nintendo to partner with Zoom and transform the boring Zoom waiting screen to a game of Dr. Mario for people to play mid-pandemic while they waited for colleagues to join the video call. We wanted a clothing brand to create a fashion show on TikTok where customers could show off the second set of clothing they purchased for wherever they were unexpectedly holed up fleeing the virus. A physically distanced birthday party in the park made me fantasize about a toilet paper brand partnering with Uber to create a summonable porta-potty to help friends extend their outdoor gathering time. When I installed a mobile horoscope app, I imagined a version produced by a healthcare provider which dished out (bad) daily wellness advice from the virus's point of view and blatant self-interest in spreading itself. (e.g., "Today you will lick the handle of a public trash can and kiss your neighbor hello.") After reading about yet another restaurant closing, I thought up a restaurant brand called Ghost Kitchen which would offer signature dishes from beloved restaurants that closed forever from COVID-19, to keep a piece of them alive.

One day at the beer store when the cashier asked for my ID, I felt ridiculous showing him my unmasked driver's license photo, which looked nothing like the masked version of myself standing in front of him. On the walk home, I imagined an adhesive brand partnering with a beer brand and producing beer can labels with peelable mask stickers for drinkers to affix to their driver's license photos and look like themselves again. The line of beer would be called "Masking Tape" and it would be a lighthearted way to remind everyone to mask up on their beer runs. And when people were feeling the discomforting side effects from their first vaccines, we thought of a beer brewed exclusively for the newly-vaxed, packed with ingredients that would help mitigate those effects, called "Cold Shot."

Coming up with these Inventions is a game you can play on your own. In the next chapter, we'll cover how to slip into the right mindset.

NOTES

1 Page, Arthur. "The Page Principles". http://page.org/site/the-page-principles

2 NCSolutions. "Butt Seriously: The TP Index" March 17, 2020. http://ncsolutions.com/covid/butt-seriously-national-tp-index/

3 Maverick. "'I Miss My Bar' Simulates the Bar Experience Through Audio" (UrbanDaddy, February 15, 2021). http://urbandaddy.com/articles/43456/i-miss-my-bar-simulates-the-bar-experience-through-audio

HABITS

"The test of a first-rate intelligence is the ability to hold two opposed ideas in the mind at the same time, and still retain the ability to function."

– *F. Scott Fitzgerald, Author*[1]

I won't tell you how to structure your day. I'm not going to say, "Meditate for 20 minutes, get eight hours of sleep and drink two cups of coffee." I don't do any of those things. But they sound really nice, so maybe I'll try them someday.

The best ideas happen as a reflex in response to a stimulus. They often spring from limited information about a problem and considering where it fits in the larger world beyond the problem.

Creativity is a habit. Here are a few habits to encourage and sharpen those reflexes.

DOI: 10.4324/9781003216872-8

Keep your antenna up for moments of friction
If you hit a snag in your daily routine – any little annoyance, disruption or frustration – ask yourself, "What would the fix to this be?" Then ask yourself, "What would each of my clients' or prospective clients' answer to that problem be? What would their take on it look like? What could they make that feels like them?"

Surround yourself with great work
The examples in this book weren't researched in one shot. They're from paying attention to standout campaigns for years. Subscribe to podcasts featuring industry leaders and learn from their creations. If you want to write a great song, you should probably listen to some Beatles. Be a forever-student. Commit yourself to lifelong learning without necessarily going back into a classroom. Then when you find or think of a great campaign …

Bag it, tag it and organize it into "moves"
Designers call this a "swipe file." I call mine, "PR A-Z." It's a running doc where you collect great ideas like rare coins. The act of writing these examples down puts them into your subconscious collection of moves. Cultivate a healthy obsession with what turns lightning bugs into lightning. But remember this habit is less about inspiration and more about setting up a collection of triggers. Being too inspired by another piece of work can result in something derivative. Being triggered by another piece of work can bring out something fresh.

Stay up on the news and trends in pop culture
Keep your eyes open. Set your cultural radar on alert. Whatever's happening in entertainment, sex, money, food, self, fashion and policy is all fodder for campaigns. Ask what product or service your brands could produce that would inject itself into one of more of these areas.

Preserve silence
Take your email offline for large chunks of the day. Do the same thing with text notifications. Make it so you can only be

reached with a phone call. Joseph Campbell said, "You must have a room, or a certain hour or so a day, where you don't know what was in the newspapers that morning, you don't know who your friends are, you don't know what you owe anybody, you don't know what anybody owes to you. This is a place where you can simply experience and bring forth what you are and what you might be. This is the place of creative incubation. At first you may find that nothing happens there. But if you have a sacred place and use it, something eventually will happen."[2]

Write within arm's reach
Keep something to write with at all times. A phone, a notepad, it doesn't matter. Yes Guitarist Trevor Rabin came up with the riff to the band's smash hit "Owner of a Lonely Heart" on a "particularly long visit" to the toilet.[3] Some of the best ideas happen in the shower. It's a place where you trade dirt for ideas. They arrive while you're waiting for your dog to finish doing her thing. It's those moments when you've forgotten about the challenge churning away in the back of your mind and become distracted with something else that an answer hits you.

Be physically active throughout the day
Whether it's walking a dog or working from a treadmill desk. Preferably both. A body in motion makes for a productive brain.

Change work locations
At least once a week, change your backdrop. Work from a park, a stoop, a courtyard, a library or a beach. You'll forget where you are, but you'll carry a feeling that something is different.

Live close to the office
Try not to have a soul-crushing commute. Paul McCartney moved into a place right by Abbey Road Studios so he could be closer to the office.[4] When you're onto something, every hour counts and you don't want to waste them getting to and from work.

Bring your well-trained dog with you

Take snuggle breaks to reset yourself and break up your tasks. Dogs also get hungry and remind you when to eat, and when to leave for the day.

Be insanely organized

It's the underpinning to a lot of this. The better-organized you are, the more your mind is freed up to wander around and find the four-leaf-clover ideas. I call it freeing up your RAM. Imagine having everything written down so you never have to remember it, and walking out your door with a clean mental slate. I once heard someone say, "As a creative, you know I'm not organized." This is a myth. I've heard it in other ways from other people, worn like a badge of honor. It's not. It's a lazy statement that implies, "I'm not as effective as I could be, if I made an effort to be better organized." Organization is a choice. It takes time, but it increases your capability. Creativity isn't an excuse for a lack of it, just like being detail-oriented isn't an excuse for not offering up original ideas.

Embrace your OCD

When you drive yourself crazy with your own OCD, it makes you want to take a wrecking ball to everything sacred and structured, for your own sanity. It makes you want to turn it all on its head and see what happens.

Understand the unity of opposites

Bruce Springsteen said, "Don't take yourself too seriously, and take yourself as seriously as death itself. Don't worry. Worry your ass off. Have ironclad confidence, but doubt – it keeps you awake and alert. Believe you are the baddest ass in town, and, you suck!"[5] That's right. You're a badass and you suck! Let it keep you awake and alert and always pushing. Marketing pro Lee Clow said to do the thing "that seems ridiculous one moment and genius the next."[6] When you have

---

Illustration 15 "The Nivea Sunslide" coated up to 100 kids per hour in SPF 50+ waterproof sunscreen

an idea and you can't decide if it's brilliant or the stupidest thing you've ever heard, that's how you know it's the one.

This was the long version I share whenever I'm asked about coming up with ideas. The short version is to stay up on the news and trends in pop culture. Surround yourself with great work. Be insanely organized. Combine that with an acute sense of the times you're living in, a deep appreciation for the world's capacity for ridiculousness, an awareness that reality isn't as solid as it appears, a realization that this whole thing is a game, the rules barely exist and cheating is allowed, a belief that anything is possible, then walk 10 miles a day on a treadmill desk and out pops an Invention in PR.

If you don't have a client who makes treadmill desks, just go for a walk.

NOTES

1 Fitzgerald, F. Scott. *The Crack-Up* (Esquire, February 1936).

2 Campbell, Joseph. *The Power of Myth* (Anchor, 1988).

3 Morse, Tim. *Yesstories: Yes In Their Own Words* (St. Martin's Griffin, 1996).

4 Barrow, Tony. *John, Paul, George, Ringo & Me: The Real Beatles Story* (Thunder's Mouth Press, 2006).

5 Springsteen, Bruce. South by Southwest keynote address (March 28, 2012). http://rollingstone.com/music/music-news/exclusive-the-complete-text-of-bruce-springsteens-sxsw-keynote-address-86379/

6 TBWA\ Los Angeles. "Disrupt Manifesto" (YouTube) http://youtu.be/hKx0IDRNfhQ

APPROACH

"Sometimes the best ideas are born alone, at home, at three in the morning, by one person."

– Karen Strauss, PR pro[1]

When we walk into a room, we bring our unique life experiences and perspectives with us. An intern on her first day at an agency could smoke an entire "creative department" with her killer idea.

The most logical idea to you may seem totally wild to someone else. That's because they're not you. They're not living in your head. Their ideas can blow your mind, too, regardless of whether either of you considers yourself creative.

Creativity is just logic from another viewpoint.

I don't consider myself creative. I think a lot of the people who go around calling themselves "creative" or "a creative"

DOI: 10.4324/9781003216872-9

are assholes. It's one of those words other people get to use to describe you, but you don't get to pin on yourself. "Innovative" is another one of those words. Brands shouldn't call themselves that either, but none of them have gotten the memo. Don't get me started.

I'm a publicist. I may go about it differently, but being a publicist is something I always respected and aspired to be, ever since my days as an intern. I'm an account person doing what any good account person does for their clients, which is doing what it takes. Working to the full extent of their ability. Being a chameleon and a Swiss Army knife. Stretching up, down and to the sides.

We can all be satisfied knowing we can produce ideas, and some of them will be viable. We can all make things that do something. That's as good as it gets.

Creativity isn't an ivory tower. It isn't restricted to people who have the word "creative" in their job title. Some companies put people in charge of fostering "cultures of creativity," which is a positive thing. But once you smack that label on someone's title, it implies to others that they're somehow superior. Don't buy it. It's in everybody.

Even knowing that, we're still afraid of scaring it away if we look at it directly or shine too bright a light on it. It's like being aware you're in a dream without startling yourself awake. Don't look it in the eye or it might run off.

So, stop thinking about it. It's less about pressuring yourself to come up with greatness and more about giving yourself something interesting to do. Ask yourself, "If I've got to sit in this office and work on a project for this brand, what would I want to spend that time doing for them?" In the context of Invention, just think about what you could make for them.

Adam Ritchie Brand Direction has an approach to campaign-building, but so does every agency. Ours is called "The Creative Compass,"[2] and what makes it a little different is the order of its elements and how they apply to Invention.

The first step is called, "**Riff.**" It's where you ask the client the usual questions about their positioning and audience. As soon as you've got a handle on who they are and who they're trying to reach, it's time to go nuts. Ignore everything you've ever done and start with a blank sheet of paper. Don't just come up with the campaign. Come up with the product. Pretend the final product doesn't even exist yet. If there's a brief, set it aside. When the client hands you a brief, it's like being handed a page from a coloring book. They want to see how you'll color it. Every time that happens, you have the power to take your crayon, start it on the page, run it off onto the table, run it onto the wall, then out the door, down the stairwell and onto the street and say, "Here's where we could go." It's always worth taking that stab. Don't give them what they ask for. Give them something they never considered. Be the agency that isn't a slave to the brief. It's not disrespectful. It's giving them the best you can possibly do for them. There are infinite ways to hit an objective.

This is part of obliterating the status quo. I call it the difference between "Basic" and "Better."

BASIC: "What does the client want?"
BETTER: "What would we like to see this brand do? What's the unexpected thing? What's the brave thing?"

BASIC: "What's the product or service?"
BETTER: "What can we make that doesn't exist: real or virtual?"

BASIC: "What's the angle in what we've got?"
BETTER: "In one move, how can we transform something everyday into something newsworthy?"

BASIC: "What media should we target?"
BETTER: "How can we experiment with a medium?"

BASIC: "How can we make news?"
BETTER: "How can we make history?"

BASIC: "What will the client think?"
BETTER: "Does it make us laugh, cry or say 'wow?'"

Making someone laugh, cry and say "wow" means going for the funny bone, the heart and the eyebrows. The best campaigns do all three.

Then talk it out with someone. Call, text or email your friends. The simple act of discussing it helps you work it out and develop it in real-time. Start as far out on the edge as you can, and work your way back toward reality. There's often a sacrificial idea, which is the first thing you come up with. It might not be viable, but now that you've cleared your throat and come up with the crazy thing, the road is open to something more doable.

If you've learned a traditional approach to PR, you might be asking yourself, "Where's the research?" This process starts with raw ideation before research. Sometimes a good idea hits you out of the blue from minimal information. It comes in a flash. A lot of academics hate this. It drives them nuts. Traditionalists like to think good ideas are only born through proper research, even though that doesn't always jibe with reality. A PR pro can come in with a great deal of category and customer knowledge, and spontaneously form the seed of a workable idea from a single prompt. A PR pro can have no category or customer experience, encounter a challenge for the first time, have an emotional reaction to it and know what to do, even if it's weird.

Good research can always lead you to an idea, and you should still do it. But not right away. You get a freebie at the very beginning. Your first instinct is often a good one, and ou only have one chance to look at something fresh for the first time. Don't squander it by retreating into research right away. It's like giving up your dribble in basketball. Give your instincts first crack at the problem. You could call it going with your gut, or you could call it an effective application of experience. You should test the viability of your ideas through research, then reshape or ditch them, but research won't always be their origin.

The approach we're laying out here is not the scientific method. I don't believe the scientific method should be the first stop on the PR train because it takes intuition out of the picture, which you can't afford to do. Don't ignore intuition. Don't fear making art. But also don't avoid research. Don't skip strategy. You can have it both ways. Public relations is an art *and* a science. If you don't prioritize the art, your target audience may ignore you. Your target audience doesn't care how you came up with the idea, and they're the only ones who matter.

So, what happens during step two, "**Research**?" This is where you turn on your cultural radar and mine for pop culture and industry trends ("secondary research") and talk to the target audience ("primary research"). Research is a hunt, and you're hunting for the gold nugget of an insight that sparks a well-informed idea. Do this, and no client can accuse you of shooting from the hip or putting all your eggs in the Riff basket. Your research doesn't have to be academic. It can be a series of conversations with the client and their target audience.

When you've got that audience member on the line, ask what else they're into and why they're into it. That's how you make your ideas cross categories. That's what gets you outside the client's same old sandbox and opens up a path to the monkey bars. If you talk to a computer geek and find out they're really into sports because of the strategy that goes into them, suddenly you're inventing a new sport in the form of a computer game that appeals to others like them. Don't think of research as

dry, crusty and boring. Think of it as, "How do I dig up that precious gold nugget of an insight that will tell me exactly what I need to make in order to appeal to these people?"

Step three, "**Refine**," is where you think about the larger issues your Invention is addressing. The best Inventions aren't self-serving stunts. They do something useful. Remember the "U" from Chapter 2 on "Types and Quality?" It doesn't have to be progressive; it just has to be useful.

Run it through a list of physical senses and see if you can make the product or service engage more than one sense.

Picture emotions like a dartboard[3] and ask yourself how many zones it can hit. Maybe your Invention pushes the brand into a completely new industry that oddly makes sense.

Then think about the rollout. Can you build in multiple calendar dates where it's relevant? Brand the ideas. Give these projects titles whose names you can see in lights. "Fearless Girl." "Boxtops for Education." "Save the Snow Day." The best campaigns sound like movie titles. The best news headlines that spring from them read like punchlines. "An Album on a Beer Can." "A Team of Pregnant Superheroes." "An Animatronic Comfort Duck." Allow them to be playful, with comedic timing and a sense of clickbait headlines which actually deliver on their promise.

Then run them through a final filter where you ask:

Is it a new category of something which never existed?

Is it the truest expression/embodiment of the brand?

Is it a desirable product/service? Would someone actually buy this?

Illustration 16 The emotional dartboard every campaign should try to hit with at least one dart

How much does the world need this? Does it fill an interesting need?

If it existed, would it earn media? Does it contain a story worth hearing? Could it win a Cannes Lion?[4]

Is this worth a chunk of my life? Will it be a pathway to living to my potential? Even when it gets impossible – and it always does – will I have moments of joy and feel like I'm on the beam?

You're making the bed you'll have to sleep in for the next six months or a year. You're signing up for a tour of duty. Make it a good one. Will it make you run to the office every day because you can't wait to keep chipping away at the next phase of it?

If you can say yes to that, you're about to do your best work.

Step four is "**Rundown,**" where you present the Invention ideas to the client. "Goldilocks" them. Put the craziest one first, the least exciting one second and the most buyable one last. Try to push the client toward the one that's a little too hot. Sometimes they'll say yes. But be prepared for them to ask you for a combination of the concepts and already start thinking about how you could make it work.

It can be a deep and lengthy process, which is why idea creation shouldn't happen on spec. Occasionally you'll have something you feel is the right idea, right off the bat. You'll be tempted to say, "Screw the rest, I'm going home and having a sandwich. Done for the day!" Sure, you can do that. But you can always improve and expand on that idea with additional thinking, conversations and time.

The word, "strategy" is nebulous and frequently misunderstood, even among experienced pros. Inventions are strategies. They boil down to "Turn an album into a beer to appeal to X," "Turn tastemakers into food to appeal to Y" and "Turn pregnant women into superheroes to appeal to Z." That's it. They don't need to be more complicated than that. Then it's only a matter of choosing the right tactics to promote what you just made.

Sometimes I'm asked if the Invention process could be automated: if a program could be written to spit out PR Inventions at the push of a button. I don't think it can be. When they say computers are coming for PR jobs, show me a computer that says, "The answer to this business challenge is taking tiny LEGO men and turning them into a perfectly scaled-down rendition of the Stonewall Uprising." I don't see computers hitting the funny bone, the chest and the eyebrows all at once. You can't quantify a concept having heart, but it's obvious when it's there and when it's not.

You could arrive at some interesting combos if you trained an AI to do it as a starting point, but the thing about a PR idea working or not comes from a very human reflex and what we consider interesting or boring, emotional or flat. Your concepts need soul and audacity to really fly.

A computer-based approach would also yield a lot of what we defined as Frivolous inventions and transformations as opposed to what we defined as Useful inventions and transformations. It might tell you to make a soap that smells like french fries, but it's not going to give you a TIME Magazine Invention of the Year like "My Special Aflac Duck." We should always strive for the Useful: concepts which solve a problem for an audience and have a reason for existing in the world.

Do that, and you'll clear the media skepticism hurdle. You'll prevent it from being shot down as "just a PR stunt," and elevate it to, "wow, look what these people came up with."

CAULIFL**O**WER

Cauliflower Crust

PIZZA

MARGHERITA PIZZA

CAULIFL**O**WER

MARGHERITA PIZZA

've kept a running doc of product inventions since college. Some of them are silly and some of them are viable. These days when I think of one on the fly, I ask myself, "What brand could or should make this?" And then I ask, "Could or should one of my clients make this?" Occasionally I'll reach out to a brand and make a suggestion. Most of the time, I post them to social media under the hashtag #InventionInPR.

The irony behind the Invention approach is if you want to promote something, you've got to make something else. If you're Fancy Feast launching a line of single-serve entrees, you need to make a cookbook for humans to eat like cats.[5] If you're Budweiser trying to promote a sustainability commitment, you need to make a soccer field out of 50,000 recycled plastic cups.[6] When you need to make two items to promote one, it feels like a lot. You're handling a twofer at that point. But if the idea and product find a home in the same invention, it lessens the burden. That's why a mix of Type 1 and Type 3 can be so efficient. Now you've got a single SKU to sell. Caulipower, the pizza with the cauliflower crust, is one of these examples. It was invented by Gail Becker. who left her post at the PR agency, Edelman, to start the company and bring her PR Invention to life.

Now that you know what goes into it, remember Invention is only one approach. Even though it's my favorite place to go first, I don't impose it on my clients if we come up with another great idea. The best idea, just like the best story, always wins.

Illustration 17   Caulipower, a pizza with a cauliflower crust, was invented by a PR pro

NOTES

1 Karen Strauss from Ketchum, in a Holmes Report Echo Chamber podcast from Cannes (June 22, 2018). Episode 120, 16:30. http://provokemedia.com/latest/podcast/article/cannes-podcast-fostering-a-culture-of-creative-collaboration (2018)

2 Adam Ritchie Brand Direction. "The Creative Compass." http://aritchbrand.com/creativecompass

3 Sigmund Freud developed the pleasure principle, which says people move toward pleasure, and away from pain. In 1980, the psychologist Robert Plutchik developed the "Wheel of Emotions." For campaign-planning, we've assimilated these into a dartboard with light and dark emotions. Every campaign must make the target audience say, "This campaign makes me feel…"

4 I joke, but every PR pro has that chance every time we step up to the plate. If you don't think your campaign would be interesting enough to win a Lion or an Anvil before you even start, maybe you should scrap it and come up with one you'd feel excited about entering. Don't worry about actually entering it and all that involves. Just worry about it being good enough that you could if you wanted to.

5 Tyler, Jordan. "New Fancy Feast cat foods inspire cookbook for cat owners" (Pet Food Processing, April 13, 2021). http://petfoodprocessing.net/articles/14643-new-fancy-feast-cat-foods-inspire-cookbook-for-cat-owners

6 Reames, Mitch. "Budweiser Recycled 50,000 Plastic Beer Cups to Make a Soccer Field in Russia" (Adweek, April 10, 2019). http://adweek.com/brand-marketing/budweiser-recycled-50000-plastic-beer-cups-to-make-a-soccer-field-in-russia/

THE CHARGE

"The job of communications professionals isn't just to put out fires, but to light them."

– *Ángel Cabrera, Educator*[1]

If there's a silent crisis happening in PR, there's also a quiet revolution. It might not be under the banner of PR because PR doesn't always wave a banner. What makes it invisible is also what makes it work.

All around us, PR minds are coming up with products and then promoting their creations. At a recent PRWeek Awards, five of the 26 categories were won by Inventions in PR.[2] I may be the first person to identify it, type it out, package it and define a firm by it. But I'm not the only one thinking about it. It's only a matter of using the tools in our arsenal to approach campaigns differently.

DOI: 10.4324/9781003216872-10

Every agency professional has had a potential client knock on their door before the product was finalized, before the service was fully baked or too long before launch time. When you go Invention-first, you'll never have to turn someone away because "it's too soon for PR" or "they're not ready for PR yet." Why put yourself at the end of the line? With Invention, there's no such thing as too early to get involved and make a valuable contribution. You can jump in right away, not just before the marketing plan comes together, but before the product roadmap is laid out.

Invention doesn't require an extraordinary amount of money or time. When we did "T.R.I.P.," the music was already finished and the beer took the same amount of time as any to prototype, brew, package and distribute. "Mix It Up" took the same effort it would take any cafe brand to expand its menu. Most of "The M.O.M. Squad's" products already existed for months, and only needed real-life avatars to unify them and make them fresh.

You also don't need an army to pull this off. You need a PR team member to drive the process, a head of marketing or CEO you've made fall in love with the idea and someone on the product team to help bring it to life. In the world of consumer packaged goods, it can be the industrial designer. In the food and beverage industry, it could be the culinary director. The rest is production, design, content creation and promotion as usual. Except by now you've loaded a silver bullet into the chamber, which you as the sharpshooter also get to fire.

Brands don't need to see themselves as daredevils to try it. The most milquetoast brands in the world are some of the best candidates. They've almost got no choice but to do something unusual if they want to make a dent in awareness.

Inspiration can come from consumer frustration, like Reese's "Candy Converter" which transformed unwanted Halloween candy into Reese's Peanut Butter Cups. It can come from consumer humor, like Fruit of the Loom's "Pillows For Posterity," which took the funniest things kids said, posted by their parents online and turned them into throw pillows. It can come from consumer passions, like the "House Wine & Cheez-It Box," a combination product created to celebrate National Wine and Cheese Day.

We need to fundamentally reject the notion of PR as a surface layer, and never allow our peers to underestimate PR's ability to create. With every campaign, we get to expand the business world's understanding of what PR can accomplish. In some ways, practicing Invention in PR is doing PR for PR.

If we see ourselves not as storytellers of what exists but as authors of what might be, we can prevent PR from being marginalized as a mouthpiece and raise its value as a creative engine worthy of greater respect. When we correct the misperception that PR is only about promotion or cleaning up a mess, we allow PR to live to its potential as a powerful inventive and transformative force that can change a brand's life.

There's no sense of ownership like conceiving an effective product which people love. It's something every PR pro should experience at least once in their career. When you drive what a brand actually makes – not just what it says – you're putting PR in charge of all functions before the campaign rubber meets the road, and gaining that ownership. Building something that represents a brand at its finest. Firing on all creative cylinders with the belief that PR can change things. Exploring the edge of our profession's final frontier.

Every marketing discipline goes to battle in what PRovoke calls the "War for Ideas." They're duking it out with the same weapons from the same manufacturers. If you enter the fight with product and service creation as your weapon, it's like jumping into a time machine and planting your flag in the ground before the first shot is fired. Invention is how the war for ideas can be won before the battle even starts.

One time I heard an agency executive talk about keeping your head down and staying in your lane, in the context of a multi-discipline team. There's something to be said for doing one thing really well. It might help you live to see another day, but you'll never leave the same old trench. And you might get hit there anyway.

There's a belief that we get stuck in our grooves as we grow older. That fresh ideas come from young minds. It doesn't have to be that way. The more experience you gain, the more you're asked to run similar campaigns to ones you've already done. You can go with what's worked in the past, or you can rebel against stagnation by throwing it out the window and trying something different, if only to keep yourself interested. You can always fall back on what worked if you need to. But going in another direction is how you get more experimental with age instead of becoming a relic.

They say nobody on their deathbed ever wished they spent more time working, but work is still an inevitable part of life. If you've got to do it anyway, wouldn't it be nice to look back and feel like it was time well spent? Invention in PR can give everyone at a company something they'll always take away from their time there. In 10 years, nobody's going to remember, "That quarter, we increased online sales by 10%." They're going to remember, "This one time, we turned pregnant ladies into comic book superheroes."

Speaking of death, you've got to love how PR keeps going from "dead" to the thing every brand eventually covets. When someone says PR is dead or dying, they mean a certain tactic out of hundreds is momentarily out of style. Just like when someone says a particular medium is dead. It's cyclical.

There are echoes of this in the unending debate about the importance of media relations, which PR professionals agonize over, even while it pays so many of our bills. Communications still relies on people, and people are imperfect and easily distracted. The exchange of information to earn exposure and mindshare remains an incredibly messy and Darwinian process. Gen Z says "Pics or it didn't happen." Business leaders say "Press or it didn't happen." There are fewer trusted outlets than ever, but it only makes whoever's left more important.

In tense situations, PR is the only professional service that helps a company walk a mile in a critic's shoes and find a way forward. Companies will always care about their image because companies will always care about profit. Saying "PR is dead" is like saying, "Business is dead."

PR will die when humans lose their natural curiosity and skepticism. When they believe everything they're told. When external validation no longer matters. None of those things are in danger of happening. They're fundamentally against human nature, and humans don't change.

You've probably heard someone say, "We're more than just a PR agency." They say, "We're a solutions agency" or something equally eye-rolling that ignores the fact that every business under the sun is a solutions provider. They'll say they help brands tell their stories. Every marketing disciple says they're in the storytelling business. What they're missing is the ability to help brands write great stories. That's what PR can and should be. It's up to us to expand the boundaries of what people believe PR can accomplish so we don't slide toward the same gray indistinguishable center as everyone else.

In this book, you've seen PR pros as authors who write brand storybooks. You've seen them as directors who film brand movies. You've seen them as producers who record brand

concept albums. We're experimenting with every medium that's ever existed, creating new ones and doing our very best work.

PR is timeless in its reinvention. It's the Madonna of careers. When we approach PR as a means of invention, we reinvent the idea of PR itself.

Every time an ad agency cleans up in a PR competition – often with an Invention in PR – hang-wringing judges say, "But PR was at the heart of the idea." That's good. And true. Let's keep acknowledging them as PR ideas. Earned-first ideas have always been held to a higher standard than paid-first ideas because the bar for what's newsworthy is so much higher than the bar for what's pasted onto a space that's been bought. Advertising is checkers and PR is chess. The advertising checkers people are learning how to play chess, but let's remember they didn't invent the game.

If you've been in the field for years and feel discouraged by PR's constant uphill battle, if you feel like so much of your job is writing emails that go unanswered and creating content that fails to engage, remember Invention is a way out of that problem.

Start with a concept. Work with a manufacturer, a cause or a relevant influencer group to make it real. Then do what PR excelled at for its first 100 years: tell the story.

Do that, and you've made the leap from communicating about things to inventing them.

The only limit to what you can invent is your own imagination and ability to attract collaborators willing to hear you out.

Illustration 18 "Fearless Girl" from State Street became a women's empowerment symbol across all industries

It's not art for art's sake. When you get it right, it's a celebration of our craft that changes what's real.

NOTES

1 Ángel Cabrera from George Mason University, quoted in a Tweet which ran in PRSA Strategies & Tactics (May 2019). The Tweet was from Cabrera's speech at the Public Relations Society of America Counselors to Higher Education 2019 Conference. http://twitter.com/sheena5427/status/1116125467860512768

2 In the 2021 PRWeek Awards, Crayola and Golin's "Crayola Colors of the World Crayons" campaign won Best Consumer Launch. Pantone and Huge's "Pantone Color of the Year 2020: A Multi-Sensory Experience" won Best in Creative Excellence and Best Promotional Event. Donate Life and the Martin Agency's "83 Futures" won Best in Multicultural Marketing. McDonald's and Golin's "Surprise Happy Meal" won Best Global Effort.

ACKNOWLEDGMENTS

"Some people do extraordinary things. Other people get credit for doing extraordinary things. The difference is who has better PR."
— *Nathalie Moar, PR pro*[1]

EDITOR

Meredith Norwich, Routledge

ILLUSTRATOR

Jennifer Leigh Salucci

ICONOGRAPHER

Jesse James Salucci, Creative Outlaw

DESIGNER

Cover design by Creative Outlaw, using Adobe Fonts "Industria" and "Franklin Gothic" and Good Ware "Robotic" icon from flaticon.com

CAMPAIGN CONTRIBUTORS

Rishava Green, The Lights Out / Matt King, The Lights Out / Jesse James Salucci, The Lights Out / Benny Grotto, Mad Oak Studios / Nick Zampiello, New Alliance East / Ben Holmes, Aeronaut Brewing Co. / Raul Gonzalez III, Aeronaut Brewing Co. / Abigail Taylor, Brooklyn Boulders / Erin Genett, Treebeard Media / Kyle Stearns / Keith Pascal, Life Alive / Leah Dubois, Life Alive / Max Pelham, Life Alive / Ron Shaich, Life Alive / Lisa Weintraub, Life Alive / Kendall Lowe, Phenomena / Kiki Mobley, Phenomena / Abigail Connor / Jen Johnson, Summer Infant / Paige Finnestad, Summer Infant / Rochelle Rosenthal, Summer Infant / Mark Messner, Summer Infant / Art Gehr, Summer Infant / Viera Boudreau / Kurt Graser, Knack Factory / Brooke Souza, Katharine Quigley and Abby Miller, Tribal Vision / Liz Aragao, Adam Ritchie Brand Direction / Leesa Coyne, Adam Ritchie Brand Direction / Kate Weiser, Adam Ritchie Brand Direction / Kelci Lowery, Adam Ritchie Brand Direction / Alexa DeVito, Adam Ritchie Brand Direction

COLLEGE TOUR

Kristin Helvey, Alaska Pacific University / Pallavi Kumar, American University School of Communication / Angie Chung and Michail Vafeiadis, Auburn University School of Communication and Journalism / Panos Panay and Ben Hogue, Berklee College of Music Institute for Creative Entrepreneurship / Kenneth Elmore, Steve Quigley and Eddie Downes, Boston University College of Communication / Jake Pehrson and Ken Plowman, Brigham Young University College of Fine Arts and Communications, School of

Communications / Loring Barnes, Bryant University / Matt Ragas, Ron Culp and Jim Motzer, DePaul University College of Communication / Jamie Ward, Eastern Michigan University Department of English Language & Literature / Rochelle Ford and Kelly Valerio, Elon University School of Communications / Brenna McCormick, Emerson College / Neil Dziemian and Cylor Spaulding, Georgetown University School of Continuing Studies / Kristian Merenda, Harvard Extension School / Jeff Morosoff, Hofstra University Lawrence Herbert School of Communication / Yvette Sterbenk, Ithaca College Roy H. Park School of Communications / Barb DeSanto, Kansas State University A.Q. Miller School of Journalism and Mass Communications Cathy Weiss, Lasell University / Tania Rosas-Moreno, Loyola University Maryland Department of Communication Keith Green, Montclair State University School of Communication and Media / Terry Fassburg, Michael Diamond and Surbhi Bir, New York University School of Professional Studies / Myo Chung, Northeastern University College of Arts, Media and Design, Department of Communication Studies / Dan Farkas, Ohio University E.W. Scripps College of Communication / Ann Marie Major and Elissa Hill, Pennsylvania State University Donald P. Bellisario College of Communications / Rachel Ravellette and Meagan Finucane, Purdue University Brian Lamb School of Communication / Alexander Laskin, Quinnipiac University School of Communications / Allison Weidhaas, Nancy Wiencek and Samantha Cepin, Rider University College of Liberal Arts and Sciences / Kautuki Jariwala, Rutgers University School of Communication and Information / Vivian Vy Lam, San Diego State University School of Journalism and Media Studies / Kristina Markos, Simmons University Department of Communications / Devyn Downs and Joerenz Tabanda-Bolina, St. John's University College of Professional Studies / Gina Luttrell, Maria Russell, Michael Meath, Brad Horn, Donna Stein, Caroline Reff, Kelly Faggin, Dennis Kinsey, Steve Masiclat, Betsy Feeley and Ulf Oesterle, Syracuse University S.I. Newhouse School of Public

Communications / Debbie Davis, Texas Tech University College of Media & Communication / Alicia Evans, The City College of New York Media & Communication Arts Department / Matt VanDyke, University of Alabama College of Communication & Information Sciences / Dawn Doty and Anna Ritz, University of Colorado Boulder College of Media, Communication and Information / Joel Nebres and Susan Grantham, University of Connecticut College of Liberal arts And Sciences / Brittany O'Connell, University of Delaware Department of Communication / Madison Behm, University of Florida College of Journalism and Communication / Brooke Hamil, University of Georgia Grady College of Journalism and Mass Communication /
Ji Young Kim, University of Hawaii at Manoa School of Communications / Kat Krtnick, University of Iowa School of Journalism and Mass Communication / Jaya Bohlmann, University of Maryland Department of Communication / Bryan Min Wang, University of Nebraska-Lincoln College of Journalism and Mass Communications / Ben Morse, University of Nevada, Las Vegas Hank Greenspun School of Journalism and Media Studies / Jensen Moore, University of Oklahoma Gaylord College of Journalism and Mass Communication / Maggie Dalton, University of South Carolina School of Journalism and Mass Communications / Loren Pickard, University of Washington Department of Communication / Mary Worley, University of Wisconsin-Eau Claire Department of Communication + Journalism / Kim Hanson, Utah Valley University Department of Communication / Jill Flanagan, Villanova University Department of Communication / Dave Philip, William Paterson University Department of Music / Jose Aviles, Wittenberg University Department of Communication

CONFERENCE TOUR

Andrea Larick and Stephanie Stahl, Content Marketing World Khyla Flores and Nic Pearce, IABC World Conference / Jason Barnhart, Sam Sims and Samantha Villegas, PRSA

International Conference / Rebecca Stone, PRSSA National Conference / Jeneen Garcia, PRSSA Leadership Assembly / Rebecca Owen and Gloria Robinson, PRSSA Northeast District Conference / Shelley and Barry Spector, The Museum of Public Relations

PRESS

Steve Barrett, Frank Washkuch, Diana Bradley and Thomas Moore, PRWeek / Paul Holmes, Aarti Shah, Diana Marszalek and Arun Sudhaman, PRovoke / Seth Arenstein, PR News / Jon Gingerich and Steve Barnes, O'Dwyer's / John Elsasser and Rod Granger, PRSA Strategies & Tactics / Richard Carufel, Bulldog Reporter / Ted Kitterman and Carlin Twedt, PR Daily / Robert and Summer Johnson, PR Nation / Mark McClennan, Ethical Voices / Amy Rosenberg, PR Talk

MENTORS

Jill Siegel, Jill Siegel Communications / Jonathan Yohannan, KIND Snacks / Carol Cone, Carol Cone On Purpose / Perry Serpa, Vicious Kid Public Relations / Steve Martin, Nasty Little Man

FAMILY

Thom, Lynn, Julie and Walter Ritchie, Esther and Bob Berman

SPECIAL THANKS

Libby Ryerson, Chris McMurry, Ben Butler, Trisha Spillane, Kathleen Rose McGovern, Brian Pagels, Greg and Anette Mansker, Barbara Hershey, Adam Lewis, Derek Sivers, Patrice Tanaka, Karen Strauss, Amanda Byrne, Katie Dadarria, Joe Vitale, Jennifer Kellas, Jen Richards and Daisy the assistant puplicist

NOTE

1 Combs Enterprises Chief Communications Officer Nathalie Moar in an interview with Sean Czarnecki, "Meet the communicator behind Sean 'Diddy' Combs' empire" (PRWeek, March 27, 2018).

ABOUT THE AUTHOR

"A leather jacket in a sea of suits."

– Katie Dadarria, Designer

Author photograph by Chris Anderson

Adam Ritchie advocates for public relations to evolve from its past as an organization's mouthpiece to its future as an organization's creative engine. Nationally regarded in the U.S., he's been named the field's most innovative professional (PRovoke), launched campaigns honored as the most creative (PRWeek) and runs a practice recognized as the top boutique agency in the country (PR News). He has won every award in the industry multiple times, presented at dozens of conferences and spoken at more than 50 universities on the topic of this book.

INDEX

For Product Safety Concerns and Information please contact our EU
representative GPSR@taylorandfrancis.com
Taylor & Francis Verlag GmbH, Kaufingerstraße 24, 80331 München, Germany

www.ingramcontent.com/pod-product-compliance
Ingram Content Group UK Ltd.
Pitfield, Milton Keynes, MK11 3LW, UK
UKHW020932180425
457613UK00013B/330